Andrea Leers

Jane Weinzapfel

Joe Pryse

Josiah Stevenson

Princeton Architectural Press · New York

MADE TO MEASURE

THE ARCHITECTURE OF

LEERS WEINZAPFEL ASSOCIATES

COMPACTING ———
& ——— WRAPPING
WEAVING ——— &
——— EMBEDDING
STITCHING ———
& ——— FITTING

1006611949

Contents

FOREWORD ———

Easy to Say, Difficult to Do

This book presents a group of buildings which, as a whole, stand out for two reasons: first, the civic nature of their programs and urban insertion, and, second, their refusal to relinquish the actual expression and innovative content of modern architecture as fragment or infill. Easy to say, difficult to do.

Careful observation of the projects shows them to be complex and varied endeavours, the results of a practice that requires perseverance to contribute to improving the city and the setting of the architecture. This may appear unambitious, but it actually requires a colossal effort at a time when the architectural profession is becoming an administrative obstacle course, where process and management seem to dominate in the interests of an effectiveness that serves only to satisfy itself. The scale of the design as a strategy in itself, in concert with context and construction techniques, is particularly evident in the work of Leers Weinzapfel Associates.

There are key themes running through an interpretation of three of the architects' buildings. Immediate context is relevant to the architects' expansion of the Harvard University Science Center. The project could be said to be a "special extrusion" from the concrete masses of the original Josep Lluís Sert building. The decision to construct these judiciously located extrusions using fragile materials allows the architects to introduce a strategy for the main building, which, despite the modest size of the intervention, highlights the large existing masses. The strategic value of infills among the masses to suggest a rereading of the original building is worthy of mention, at a time when the modern architecture of the heroic period needs this kind of meticulous intervention to avoid being relegated to the depot of useless monuments.

Architecture as a geographical order comes under the spotlight with the University of Pennsylvania Gateway Complex in Philadelphia. The project highlights the integration of two programs—one infrastructural, the other athletic—that improves the urban space and gives new meaning to the space of the sports facility. The integration serves to free the plant of the negative content normally associated with this kind of facility. By producing such hybrids, it is possible to create new images and introduce new ways of generating spaces.

The architects worked with enveloping techniques to realize a new building for Harvard University Library Services within the historic fabric of Cambridge's Harvard Square. Wrapped in glass and terracotta, it responds differently to the conditions of the site: At certain times gently reflecting its surroundings, at others emanating a light that illuminates it, the building stands as a structure that is open to potential users and to the voyeurs who happen upon it.

The experiences presented in the book can be seen as a set of innovative notions for the construction of a space that is capable of creating a better environment. Again, easy to say, difficult to do.

Joan Busquets

PREFACE————————

Transformative Measures

Leers Weinzapfel Associates is a practice invested in the optimistic premise that architecture is most potent when it is immersed in the conflicts and tensions inherent in the social, cultural, and economic conditions that shape the built environment. The architects' work, philosophically and physically, often finds its generative material and greatest strength at the intersection of such complex variables. For twenty-eight years, the firm has created architecture from unpromising conditions, from Gordian knots of existing buildings and infrastructure, bringing public life and identity to sites and structures that had previously existed in isolation.

Andrea Leers and Jane Weinzapfel began their collaborative practice in 1982. Though raised in different parts of the country, their backgrounds and formal training share common values and lineages. Andrea Leers studied architecture at the University of Pennsylvania, where Louis Kahn's studios were informal, school-wide experiences. Jane Weinzapfel, the daughter of a builder, brought a unique appreciation of the physical and material potential of architecture with her to the University of Arizona. There her professors, former students of Louis Kahn, applied his values to their teaching. While many of the elite universities at that time were actively investigating the expressive potential of building systems, Kahn was intent on giving value and formal expression to a higher vision, to the more synthetic potential of architecture. He envisioned a resonance between the systemic logics of structural and mechanical obligations with the poetry of light, place, and clarity of material expression. Both Leers and Weinzapfel initiated their professional apprenticeships sharing Kahn's intensity of inquiry and his openness to discovering the profound within the mundane. It is not surprising that both Leers and Weinzapfel found much in common when they first worked together in the office of Cambridge, Massachusetts–based architect Earl Flansburgh, and years later when they established their own office.

Early in their practice, Leers and Weinzapfel sought commissions that their contemporaries ignored. Infrastructure projects were deemed the province of engineers and, indeed, clients expected very little from architects on such projects. When they were asked to renovate a support facility for tollbooth collection and maintenance operations at Boston's Tobin Bridge, the architects looked closely at the existing building, a provisional box suspended from the underside of the steel structure crossing the city's Route 1, and saw the potential of bringing visibility to what was unseen. Leveraging the open vistas afforded by the 120-foot-high elevation, the architects heightened the distinctions between inside and outside, announced the structure's utilitarian clarity with a red-painted steel frame, and brightened the dark interior with natural light filtered through perimeter glass-block panels. This project was a seminal contemporary example of transforming infrastructure into architecture, a process with the potential to convert the single-use functionalism of roadways and bridges into foundations for new forms of inhabitation.

More recently, the firm's design for the University of Pennsylvania Gateway Complex utilized an inverse strategy to the acupuncture-like collaboration with the Tobin Bridge. The chiller plant, located in a highly visible but ill-defined site at the edge of the campus, had the dual challenge of housing massively scaled cooling equipment while creating a new landmark gateway to the university. Competing with a nearby river and network of roadways and recreational fields, the project required an equally large-scale presence to command a legible identity. The architects recognized the necessity of the infrastructure and river by creating an equally bold gesture. Adding a super-scaled, self-contained elliptical form to this landscape, a continuous scrim of metal mesh reveals and frames the cooling equipment inside. The simple and powerful gesture of this giant ellipse, when illuminated at night, defines an ephemerally provocative new landmark for the campus.

Study of building from below, Tobin Bridge Administration Building,
Boston, Massachusetts, 1981

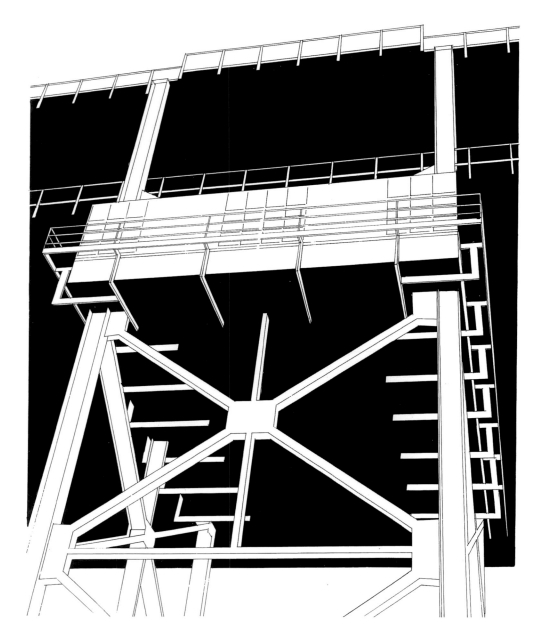

These strategically divergent approaches to designing infrastructural projects also characterize their approach to institutional projects. Just as the Tobin Bridge yielded to the architects' transformational alterations, they also see outdated campus structures as opportunities for evolutionary change.

At Smith College, the administration and trustees were committed to creating a new identity for their fitness center and offered the architects sites that could accommodate freestanding structures. Instead, the architects opted for a stealth approach, electing to unite two well-located but outdated gymnasiums, inconveniently separated by a steep slope, into one fully connected entity. In contrast to the adjacent opaque and gravity-bound brick structures, the architects introduced an elegant and crisply detailed multistory glass bridge that links the two buildings, making legible the previously unseen activities of the existing gymnasia and establishing programmatic continuity where none had existed.

The deft choreography Leers Weinzapfel Associates brought to the design of the Smith College Fitness Center is in full evidence at Harvard University, where the architects encountered different forms of resistance in buildings with radically different heritages. Challenged to introduce a state-of-the-art theater into the university's nineteenth-century Hasty Pudding Club, the architects faced the potential problem of the python swallowing the elephant. The intimately scaled historic structure resisted accommodation of thirty thousand square feet of volumetrically demanding new program, so the architects chose to preserve the existing structure while doubling its size with a modern volume. The addition, virtually invisible from the street, introduces new pathways and connections into the New College Theatre and through the campus.

Strategic additions to university buildings are necessary to support each institution's growth; giving existing buildings room to breathe often requires radically different strategies. Though the architects' design for the New College Theatre benefited from an oppositional strategy, distinguishing new from old, their design for the expansion of Josep Lluís Sert's heroic Science Center at Harvard offers an entirely different but equally proactive approach. Here, Sert's dynamic aggregate-concrete volumes eschewed easy adaptation. But the architects' gift for collaboration is in full evidence with the expansion of this modernist giant. The introduction of sixty-five thousand square feet of program into this self-contained building was accomplished with a perimeter pinwheel of glass additions. Anchored on the foundation of the existing opaque structure, the additions of clear and diffused glass volumes form a seemingly effortless evolution of the iconic original. Following the meter and proportion of the existing concrete and glass elements of the original building, the finer grain of the channel glass follows the taut geometric cues of the existing building, while infusing it with a quality of luminosity it never possessed. Like the best of collaborations, the additions benefit from the formal strength of the original structure, but perhaps most importantly, the science departments, and indeed Harvard's campus, benefit from the transformation of a twentieth-century landmark into a compelling symbol of contemporary campus life.

Leers Weinzapfel Associates' work reveals a commitment to the clarity of form and the active engagement in social discourse that modernism offers, while also exploring innovative responses to changing physical and cultural contexts. Avoiding the cliché that creativity in design can only emerge with complete freedom from everyday constraints, the work achieves resonance through its situation within the social, political, circum-stantial, technological, and economic frameworks that define each project. Through the act of design, the architects seek to construct new identities for each situation, inventively engaging with the sites and programs they transform.

Marion Weiss

INTRODUCTION—

An Architecture of the Good Fit

This is a book about the work we have built, and the intentions that shaped it. It is about testing ideas in tangible form, about beginning with the general and ending with the particular. It is about making spaces for human occupancy and social exchange, buildings inspired and constrained by site and setting, and architecture experienced through encounters with materiality.

Good architecture is like good tailoring. It is about making and constructing. It is about material, its assembly, and detail—the tactile and sensual means by which architecture is experienced. It is about measure and the concepts of precision, proportion, and adjustment. It is about form, shape, and silhouette. Architecture must find the fit for its purpose, its role in the ensemble, its size, and its scale. Each of the projects discussed here reflects our commitment to the fabric from which it emerged, the ways in which it is woven into the site, and how it is stitched and fitted into the larger life of the city or the campus. The goal of our architecture is to find a tailor-made response to each set of conditions—a response that conveys both conceptual consistency and specific character.

Administration Building suspended under the bridge and toll plaza, Tobin Bridge
Administration Building, Boston, Massachusetts, 1991

Our practice began with a series of urban infrastructure projects. The exceptional technical demands, coupled with strictly utilitarian programs, prompted fresh thinking. The Tobin Bridge Administration Building in Boston involved the full renovation of a structure suspended 120 feet above the ground. In a nearby suburb, a snowplow garage and maintenance building for the Hanscom Field regional airport prioritized sustainable design with its fully glazed, south-facing wall of roll-up doors.

The unusual design challenges of our early work led to a number of even more demanding and highly visible civic and community buildings. These technically complex projects are built upon or woven into existing structures and embedded in the urban fabric. The human purposes and programs for these buildings are similarly complex. Distinctions between public and private realms are blurred; the space for human activities and the space of technology and infrastructure are commingled. Constructional systems are a blend of craft and industrial technique, employing materials that are heavy and light, ancient and modern. Together these projects constitute a creative collection of hybrid buildings based on composite conditions.

Detail at roll up doors and snow-melting hot air blowers, Hanscom Field Maintenance Building, Bedford, Massachusetts, 1983

Executive offices cap the MBTA Operations Control Center, Boston, Massachusetts, 1993

Three-story addition reads as giant bay window, U.S. District Courthouse, Worcester, Massachusetts, 1995

In downtown Boston, the ten-story Operations Control Center for the city's subway system reuses the framework of an existing five-story building to house expanded facilities. In Worcester, Massachusetts, a tier of new courtrooms inserted in the upper-level light well of a 1930s federal building converts the structure into a state-of-the-art U.S. District Courthouse. In the former industrial city of Lawrence, Massachusetts, a new judicial center joins the powerful mill buildings and canal district to the civic center. A series of youth recreation centers in Boston, all created with active community participation and on minimal budgets, reimagines and extends inadequate existing structures.

Brick portico lines industrial canal with projected metal clad volume marking the corner entry, Fenton Judicial Center, Lawrence, Massachusetts, 1998

Vaulted gymnasium gives teen area a distinct identity, George R. White Gymnasium and Teen Center, South Boston, Massachusetts, 1991

More recently, the challenge of fitting into existing infrastructure and complex urban environments led us to think similarly about building in the ensemble of campus and university settings. Once again, constrained sites, no site, or sites between disparate elements were the occasions to think about the possibilities of weaving, embedding, and fitting a new structure into the ensemble. At the University of North Carolina at Chapel Hill, the Global Education Center takes advantage of a steeply sloped site and a grove of mature trees to create a transition between large-scale institutional structures on one side and intimate domestic-scale structures on the other.

Offices float above a glazed ground floor with the Commons marked by vertical louvers opening onto a shady terrace. University of North Carolina at Chapel Hill Global Education Center, Chapel Hill, North Carolina, 2007

An Evolving Strategy

With a desire to create meaningful places for social interaction and a passion for material exploration, we begin with the facts on the ground. A reading of the site—its history, microclimate, orientation, topography, ground conditions, and natural resources, together with surrounding structures and infrastructures—is our point of departure. A deep understanding of the site suggests ways to use resources and energy wisely. In contrast to a preconceived formal strategy, we look for an alignment between the nature and size of the program, the palette of materials, and the salient characteristics of the site. We look for a fit between the identity of our intervention and the ensemble.

Three essential strategies have emerged from this process, each helping to take account of how the purposes of program are inflected by the particularities of place: *Compacting & Wrapping*, *Weaving & Embedding*, and *Stitching & Fitting*.

In identifying these approaches, we do not suggest that this document is a comprehensive view of the projects, but rather a focused lens through which to observe the process of design. Like all good tailoring, our goal is an architecture made to fit a particular purpose and set of conditions, made with style, skill, and precision, and made to last.

COMPACTING & WRAPPING

Across the country, well-established campuses face a series of critical challenges that stand in the way of their growth. Larger demographic trends and the explosion of student enrollment through 2009, changing learning environments, and the increasing importance of student life facilities all place great pressures on the future development of college campuses. Adequate sites for new buildings are scarce, as pressures to contain the campus within the surrounding community grow, and universities are increasingly demolishing existing buildings to make way for new ones.

The infrastructure equipment necessary for this growth is especially problematic, as its size and inaccessibility make it an unwelcome insertion in the fabric of a campus. Similarly problematic and equally important to the quality of campus life are nonacademic structures such as campus centers, recreation centers, and administrative service centers, which must be centrally located. These combined pressures lead to the common situation of introducing a building too large or too prominent for its site.

The following examples demonstrate how dense, compact, freestanding objects can accommodate very large, but different, programs on small sites. Internal subdivision rather than additive assembly produces differentiated spaces, allowing the envelope of these buildings to become the primary focus of study. Each is a tautly wrapped container with a clear shape and continuous, compact form. The choice of material, articulation and detail, texture, transparency, and strategies for entries and openings are all intensely important to the legibility of these substantial structures.

An elliptical metal screen wall encloses
rectilinear glazed walls of the chiller plant
building and truck turning areas.

University of Pennsylvania Gateway Complex

Philadelphia, Pennsylvania, 2000

The need for increased chilled-water capacity to serve a growing campus prompted the University of Pennsylvania to plan a new facility in a highly visible location in West Philadelphia along the Schuylkill River at the University Avenue Bridge. The site, previously used for athletic fields, was one of the few remaining open spaces on campus large enough to accommodate the new structure. In order to explore how this large infrastructure installation could be an attractive gateway presence, while retaining maximum use of the site for a baseball field and other athletic activities, the university conducted an invited design competition. This project was the winning entry.

The site is a virtual island, a lozenge-shaped parcel at the edge of the campus defined by a bend in the river, major roadways, and a railroad right-of-way. It is cut off from the regular street grid and has only one entry at its western end. Grassy berms protect its edges, creating a bowl at the interior of the site with a positive sense of enclosure.

The sixty-thousand-square-foot footprint of the chiller-plant equipment building and the specific shape and orientation of the baseball field required a combined building and site concept. Wrapping the rectangular chiller plant with a continuous screen-wall in a fluid elliptical form offers a unique solution. The compact elliptical form adjusts to the curves of the river and roads with no distinct "face," following along the site boundary to make room for the baseball field. By extending the screen enclosure beyond the boundaries of the plant itself, vehicle service areas are contained at the two ends of the structure and the plant inside can be built in phases. The remaining portion of the site is free of vehicles for the full development of athletic activities. As an added benefit, the dimensions of the elliptical enclosure are the same as those of a quarter-mile jogging track. The position of the chiller plant allows an optimal playing orientation for the baseball field; its nine-hundred-seat grandstand and press box, anchored in an earth berm, offer a dramatic view of the city. Behind the baseball field and chiller plant, a dense screen of trees buffers the railroad tracks from the active green space of the site. The two large elements are thus nested together within the constraints of the parcel to create an optimal setting for each.

Study of the screen wall and its relationship to the body of the building it wraps was the subject of intense research to develop a cost-effective, durable, maintainable system. The sixty-foot-high screen-wall is composed of perforated stainless steel panels, corrugated for stiffness, and attached to a steel framework of columns, beams, and subframes. Lateral bracing tied to the equipment building, or diagonal bracing beyond the building secured at the ground, stabilizes the giant screen-wall. The inner equipment building is clad in glass curtain wall on the long face to the river and opaque metal insulated panels on the opposite side. The ends of the building have roll-up glass doors, which allow vehicles to drive through the facility from one service area to the other. Inside, the equipment is color coded in bright greens, blues, and violets to dramatize its presence and to denote its respective functions. The space between inner building and screen wall is partly occupied on the enclosed side of the building by support and concession space for the athletic facilities and left open on the glazed side of the building. Interior lighting illuminates colorful equipment at night, and a crown of extended lights at the top of the screen wall gently washes the enclosure to reveal the complete form of the ellipse while emitting light from within.

The screen wall around the chiller plant celebrates the industrial nature of the structure and gives it a distinct identity. The screen veils the building, making it a shimmering, silvery object by day, and reveals the rooftop chillers above. By night, the building becomes a translucent glowing object, partially exposing the equipment within. Due to its substantial size, distinctive form, and mysterious translucency, the chiller plant is recognizable from major roadways and from across the river. Set in a vibrant green landscape along the river, it is a memorable gateway to the campus.

Campus plan

The irregularly shaped site,
containing the separate chiller plant
and baseball field precincts,
is surrounded by river, roadways,
and railroad tracks.

© Peter Aaron / Esto

→ Approached from University
Bridge, the screened enclosure of
the chiller plant precinct provides
a gateway presence to the University
at the river's industrial edge.

© Peter Aaron / Esto

↘ At night the illuminated screen wall
emphasizes the southern gateway to
the University from the bridge.

© Peter Aaron / Esto

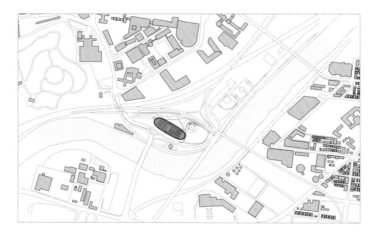

University of Pennsylvania Gateway Complex

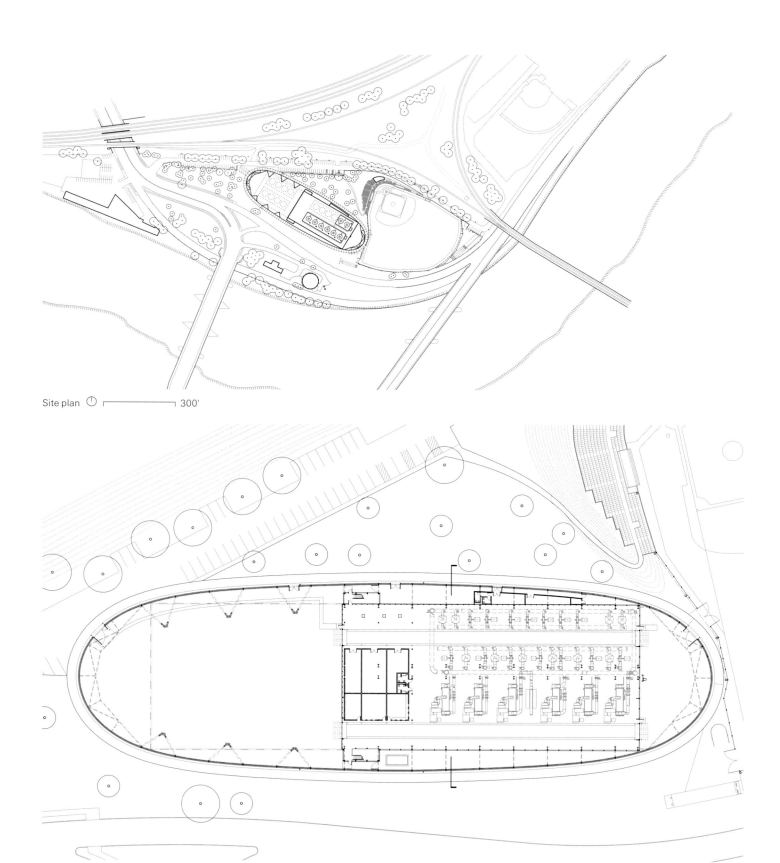

Site plan   ⏲   ⊢⎯⎯⎯⎯⎯⎯⎯⎯⎯⊣ 300'

Ground-floor plan, first phase–second phase dotted in.   ⏲   ⊢⎯⎯⎯⎯⎯⎯⎯⎯⎯⊣ 60'

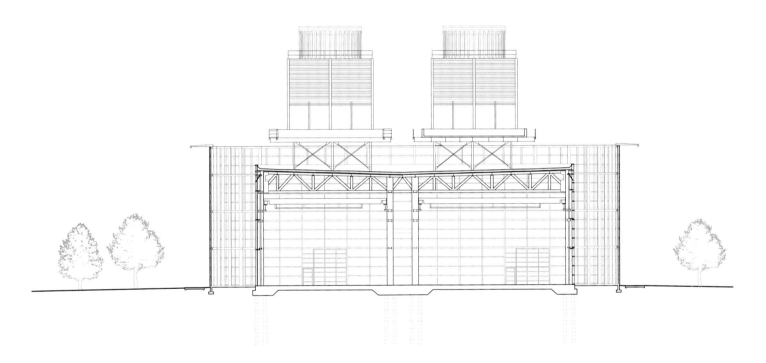

Building section ⌐━━━┐ 20'

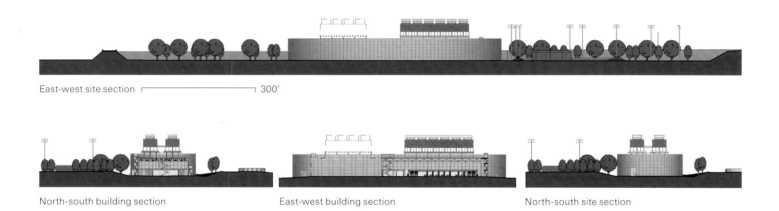

East-west site section ⊢————————⊣ 300'

North-south building section   East-west building section   North-south site section

University of Pennsylvania Gateway Complex

← A system of primary and
secondary steel supports the
screen wall panels with horizontal
trussed lateral bracing near the
top of the enclosure.
© Peter Aaron / Esto

Screen wall detail model

The custom corrugated perforated
stainless steel panel designed to form
the light screen wall enclosure has
since become available as a standard
manufactured product.
© Peter Aaron / Esto

Screen wall study model

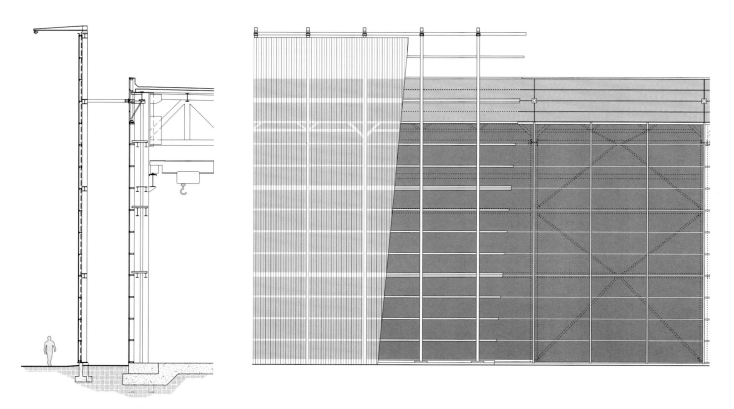

Screen wall and building wall detail ⌐――――――⌐ 16'

Chiller equipment, crane rail, and
traffic ways are color coded for safety.

A series of glass bi-fold garage doors
provide truck access through the
building with turn around space
within the screen wall.
© Peter Aaron / Esto

Perimeter lighting is directed at
a precise angle to wash the top part
of the screen wall while leaving the
lower portion transparent to the view
of interior equipment.
© Peter Aaron / Esto

Princeton University Chilled Water Plant Expansion

Princeton, New Jersey, 2006

Princeton University required an expansion of its existing chilled-water plant at a highly visible location along Elm Drive, the major vehicular entrance to the center of campus. The university also needed to find a location for a large thermal-energy, water storage tank in a nearby location.

Design began with the development of a master plan for the service precinct, which included the existing cogeneration plant, chilled-water plant, cooling towers, parking, and the new expansion elements. The plan documented a phased strategy to increase the physical plant facility and capacity over the next twenty years, consistent with the larger goals of campus planning. Locations for future chillers and cooling towers and a thermal-energy, water storage tank, sized for future growth, were identified. A strategy was developed that used the existing chilled-water plant roof as a site for the numerous future cooling towers that would be needed for the central campus. Structure was sleeved through this existing building to support the new equipment. Siting for the new chiller-plant expansion was developed to consolidate required service and piping for the long-term project, as well as to screen the impact of large new equipment and unattractive existing structures from the rest of the campus.

The first design phase included adding new chillers within a new building, adding new cooling towers atop the existing plant, and building the water storage tank, which was sized for the final phase. The new chiller plant is conceived as a compact, rectangular volume that acts as a shield for the growing service area. Its public faces are consistent with the high quality of buildings throughout the campus, and the height of its walls helps to screen future cooling towers from view.

Oriented perpendicular to the end of the existing chiller plant, the new building has a long stone wall parallel to the campus road and two projected end-walls of translucent glazing. The structure takes advantage of the sloping site to create service access to the building's mezzanine at one end, and the ground floor at the other end.

The stone chosen for the forty-foot-high, ninety-foot-long wall facing the campus is local schist, similar to the cleft argillite stone used in the many collegiate gothic campus structures. The schist stone is grayer than argillite and laid in an irregular ashlar pattern to create an overall textured plane of material. The new wall is more abstract than the typical stone campus buildings, but nevertheless creates a strong relationship with them. Glazing at the two projected building ends is a rich composition of translucent glass for equipment areas and fritted glass for staff areas. The continuous roof-edge at the juncture of the ends of the stone wall and recessed corner glazing emphasize the compact volume and articulated details. On the uphill end, equipment is hoisted onto the mezzanine through a single fold-up glazed overhead door. On the downhill end, similar, but larger, multiple doors allow full vehicle access to large chiller equipment. Operable windows and overhead doors at each end provide flow-through ventilation for staff comfort.

The new thermal-energy, water storage tank is a cylindrical form deeply embedded in the sloping site to minimize its height. Its powerful shape and size, wrapped in ribbed metal siding, can be glimpsed through trees along Elm Drive.

← The glazed curtain wall system is composed of translucent glass in equipment areas and fritted glass in staff areas, fold-up equipment doors, and view-height operable windows.
© Alan Karchmer / Esto

Campus plan

Facilities plant precinct
master plan

→ The uphill side of the translucent glazed face of the new chiller plant building provides entrance to a staff mezzanine at ground level and maintenance access to the upper equipment floor, while screening rooftop equipment added to the existing building beyond.

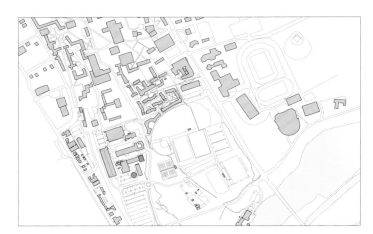

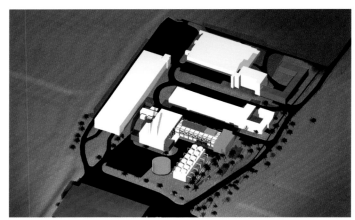

← The downhill translucent glazed face of the new chiller plant provides truck access to three tall ground-floor chiller bays and operable windows in the upper equipment floor.
© Alan Karchmer / Esto

↙ Color-coded equipment and fritted glass at eye level enlivens the interior.
© Alan Karchmer / Esto

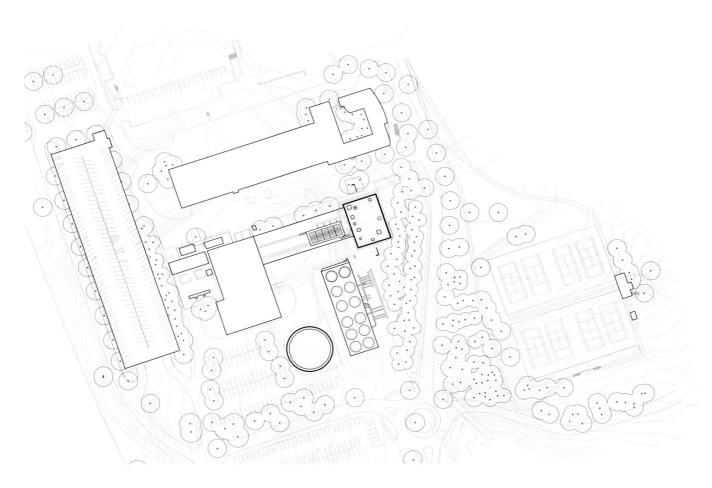

Site plan ⊕ ⊢———————┐ 200'

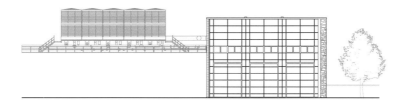

South elevation

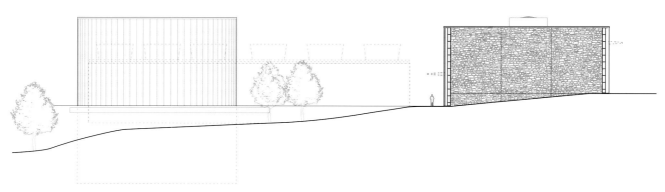

East elevation

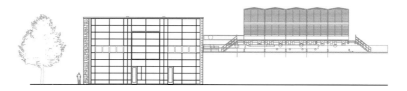

North elevation ⊢————⊣ 40'

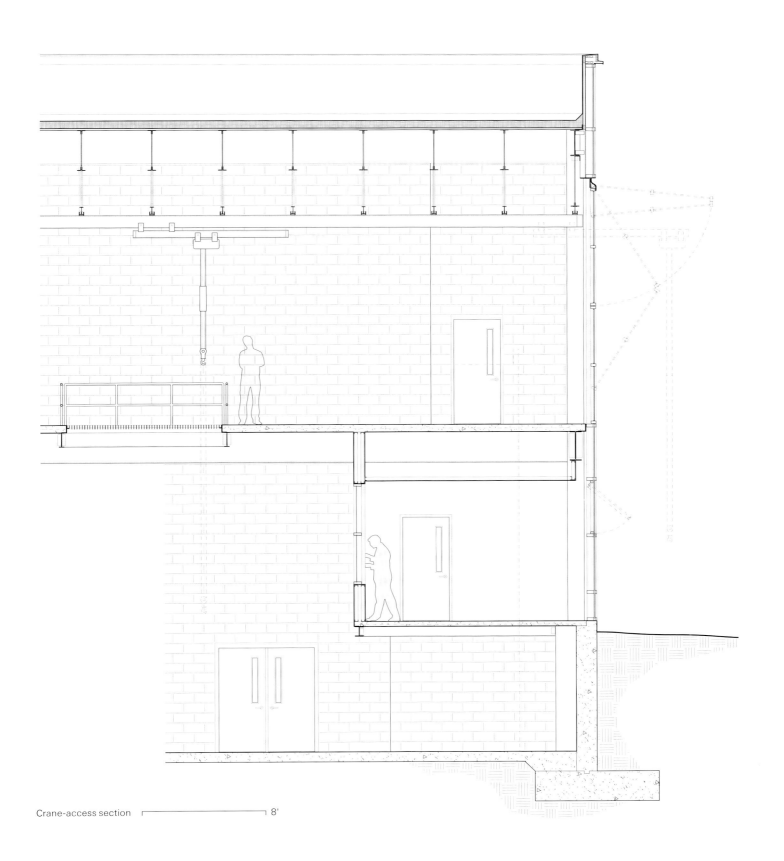

Crane-access section ⊢——————⊣ 8'

The taut curtain-wall system of
the short end walls contrasts with
the rough schist stone of the long
street-side wall.

University of Cincinnati University Pavilion

Cincinnati, Ohio, 2003

In support of campus master-planning goals, the University of Cincinnati wished to bring together admissions, enrollment, financial aid, the registrar, the bursar, career development, educational services, disability services, and a new visitor center into a user-friendly, "one-stop" building at the heart of the campus. The site on McMicken Commons, the historic center of campus, was occupied by a small academic building, which was to be demolished to make way for the much larger University Pavilion. Sloping more than thirty feet from the academic ridge to the lower ravine, the site is surrounded by some of the most significant structures on campus, including the original 1948 McMicken Hall, whose roofline established the height limit for the new building. Entries and connections from the University Pavilion to adjacent buildings on several levels were desired. Constrained on all sides and in its height, the site set a significant challenge for its new program.

A compact, six-story rectangular volume of simple strength embedded in the steep slope, the building forms a clear boundary to the commons and defines a new campus entry plaza. The long side of the building facing the commons is conceived as a "window on the campus," alive with activity and movement between several levels and entrances. An upper-level entrance at the visitor center acts as a front door for the campus and the admissions department. A midlevel entrance from the commons leads directly to the One Stop Student Service Center, with a large open space containing flexible meeting pods for assistance with online registration, financial aid, and other transactions. A lower-level entrance allows access to the frequently visited departments for career development and educational and tutoring services from a nearby parking structure. The top floor of the building, which houses the offices of the president and senior administrators, is surrounded by a loggia, reducing the reading of the volume to five stories.

Closely coordinated with the campus landscape master-plan, an exterior stair descends the slope to connect upper and lower campuses. Inside the building, a broad stairway within the atrium zone parallels the exterior steps. Together, the exterior and interior stairs form a welcome campus passage in fair or inclement weather. On the upper three office floors, meeting rooms extend into the atrium, and at the roof level, an observation terrace overlooking the commons provides a crown for the building, a destination for visitors, and a venue for campus functions. Beyond the atrium, a largely open office area on each floor offers maximum flexibility and enjoys light from all sides of the building.

Because of the size and density of the new building, careful selection of exterior materials was essential to avoid a heavy and overwhelming presence. Relatively smaller in scale, surrounding buildings are largely clad in brick and limestone. A strategy of snugly wrapping the building in two contrasting materials proved to be an effective solution. On the east, west, and south facades, a rose-colored Alabama limestone veneer encloses the dense and compact form and relates to the masonry ensemble of nearby buildings. On the south facade, sunscreen and light shelves introduce reflected light deep into the interior workspaces while shielding ribbon windows from direct sunlight. By contrast, the north facade, which overlooks the commons, takes advantage of its orientation and the generous exterior space to provide maximum daylight through a continuous glazed-wall, which turns at both corners. Trellislike framing gives alternating clear, fritted, and translucent glass panels an overall texture and continuity. The only elements to punctuate the taut volume are the entry vestibules at each of three lower levels, marked by red metal canopies, red panels, or red fritted glass.

Interior materials reflect the enclosure strategy. The rear wall of the atrium is made of a red, aniline-dyed plywood, providing a solid backdrop for the light wood railings and the conference-room screen that curves into the atrium. Flooring in the atrium on the stairs is a rosa verona marble corresponding to the carnelian granite on the exterior site steps. Seen across the commons at night, the building glows with light, color, and activity.

Campus plan

Site and height limits diagram

The University Pavilion frames
one end of the central McMicken
Commons.

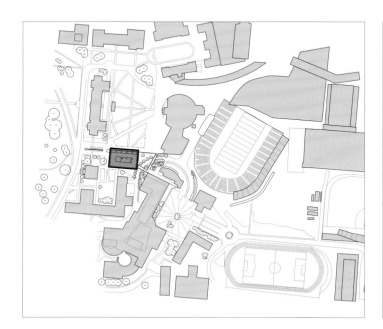
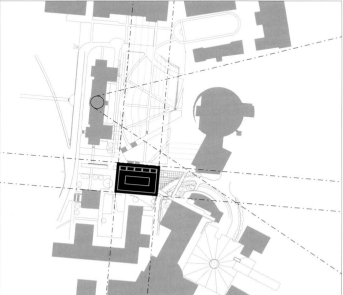

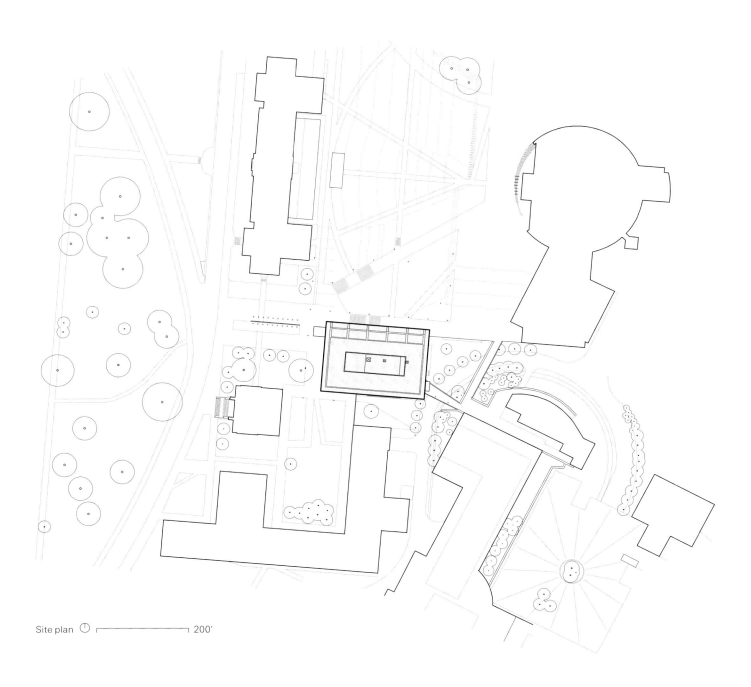

Site plan 200'

Cross section perspective

→ Fritted, clear and red glass, and a lattice of mullions animate the north-facing window on the campus.
© Alan Karchmer / Esto

↘ A bridge to adjacent buildings and a lower level garden entrance support connections from the upper levels of McMicken Commons to the lower ravine area of the campus.
© Peter Aaron / Esto

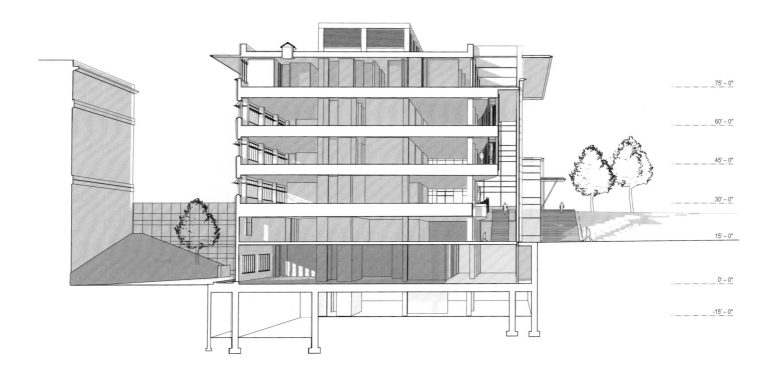

75' – 0"

60' – 0"

45' – 0"

30' – 0"

15' – 0"

0' – 0"

-15' – 0"

University of Cincinnati University Pavilion

→ The main visitor entry is located on the upper McMicken Commons level and is visible from the central campus entry drive.

© Peter Aaron / Esto

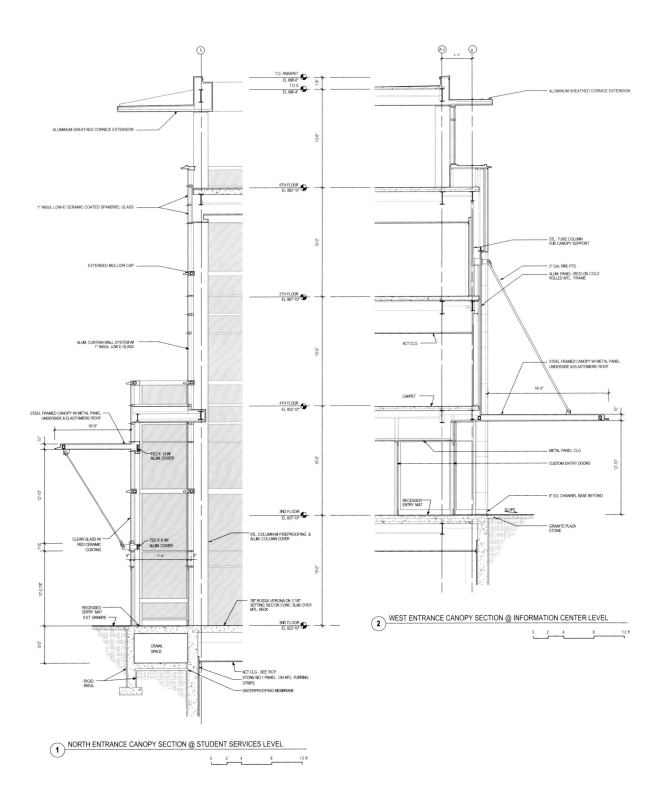

ALUMINUM SHEATHED CORNICE EXTENSION

ALUMINUM SHEATHED CORNICE EXTENSION

1" INSUL LOW-E CERAMIC COATED SPANDREL GLASS

STL. TUBE COLUMN FOR CANOPY SUPPORT

EXTENDED MULLION CAP

2" DIA. PIPE PTD.

ALUM. PANEL (RED) ON COLD ROLLED MTL. FRAME

ALUM. CURTAIN WALL SYSTEM W/ 1" INSUL LOW E GLASS

ACT CLG.

STEEL FRAMED CANOPY W/ METAL PANEL UNDERSIDE & ELASTOMERIC ROOF

CARPET

STEEL FRAMED CANOPY W/ METAL PANEL UNDERSIDE & ELASTOMERIC ROOF

TS2 X 12 W/ ALUM. COVER

METAL PANEL CLG.

CUSTOM ENTRY DOORS

CLEAR GLASS W/ RED CERAMIC COATING

8" S.S. CHANNEL BASE BEYOND

TS2 X 6 W/ ALUM. COVER

RECESSED ENTRY MAT

STL. COLUMN W/ FIREPROOFING & ALUM. COLUMN COVER

SLOPE

GRANITE PLAZA STONE

7/8" ROSSA VERONA ON 2 1/8" SETTING BED ON CONC. SLAB OVER MTL. DECK

RECESSED ENTRY MAT EXT. GRANITE

CRAWL SPACE

RIGID INSUL

ACT CLG - SEE RCP

STONE NO. 1 PANEL ON MTL. FURRING STRIPS

WATERPROOFING MEMBRANE

T.O. PARAPET EL 898'-0"
T.O.S. EL 896'-4"
6TH FLOOR EL 882'-10"
5TH FLOOR EL 867'-10"
4TH FLOOR EL 852'-10"
3RD FLOOR EL 837'-10"
2ND FLOOR EL 822'-10"

2 WEST ENTRANCE CANOPY SECTION @ INFORMATION CENTER LEVEL

0 2 4   8   12 ft

1 NORTH ENTRANCE CANOPY SECTION @ STUDENT SERVICES LEVEL

0 2 4   8   12 ft

The interior lobby stair parallels
the broad site stair and landscape
beyond.
© Peter Aaron / Esto

→ Viewed from the visitor entry,
the vertical lobby connects five
interior levels with a view through the
window onto the campus
© Peter Aaron / Esto

The career development suite
at the lower garden level is visually
connected to the lobby above.
© Peter Aaron / Esto

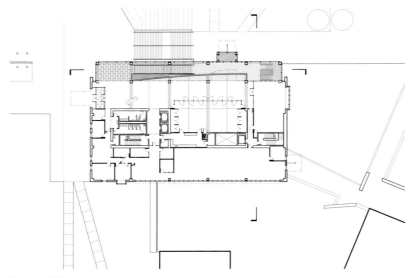

Plaza and Visitor Center entry-level plan

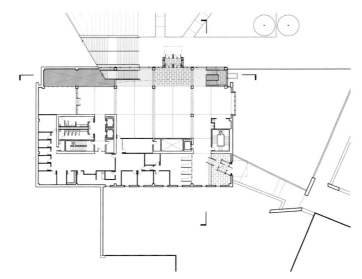

Commons and Student Center entry-level plan

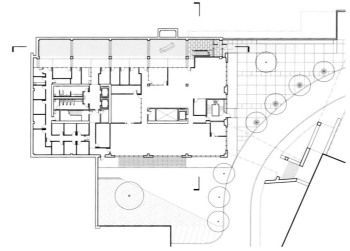

Lower drive and garden-level plan ⊕ ⌐————————⌐ 60'

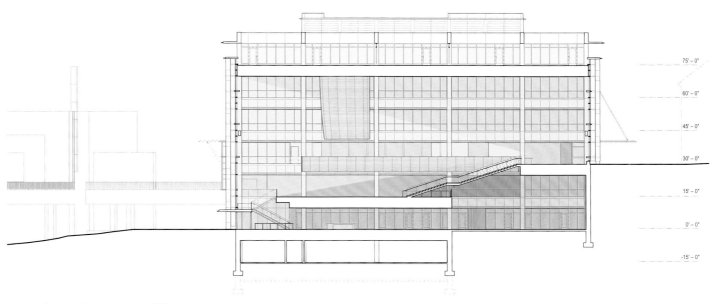

75' – 0"

60' – 0"

45' – 0"

30' – 0"

15' – 0"

0' – 0"

-15' – 0"

Longitudinal section ⌐——⌐ 20'

WEAVING & EMBEDDING

Sometimes the best site is no site at all. In dense urban centers or fully built campuses, new programs must be inserted as fragments woven into the living fabric of the ensemble. The need for a program to be expanded in its existing location, a new activity to be inserted in a critical position, or a better use to be developed in place of the old requires ingenuity in finding space where there appears to be none. However, the constraint of no site can be an opportunity to add to a dynamic patchwork of building over time, with each addition contributing to a larger, more coherent whole. The technical challenges of weaving new construction into, on top of, or within existing structures are formidable, often requiring more structural and systems rethinking than designing a freestanding building. Issues of form, scale, and material are essential to the integration of embedded elements.

A careful reading of the surrounding fabric can lead to several strategies for a new intervention and composite form. Perched on top, nestled in between, attached alongside, or reclaimed within, new spaces can be embedded into already complex physical frameworks. Where the established structural system is repetitive and flexible, it can be reinhabited with new forms and spaces. Where the existing buildings are formally complex or diverse, strong and minimal new volumes may be most legible by contrast. Where heavy masonry materials are predominant on the site, new spaces may be glazed and transparent. The use of constant scale elements, such as windows or panel sizes, can bridge between contrasting forms and materials.

New colorful metal-framed meeting room
joins existing vaulted structure, enclosed
for activities, and new gymnasium

62

Blue Hill Avenue Youth Development Center

Boston, Massachusetts, 1995

To serve a densely populated and multiracial urban neighborhood, the City of Boston partnered with the Boys and Girls Clubs of Boston to build a new recreation, social, and learning center for young people on the site of an abandoned ice hockey rink. The center provides a safe and welcoming after-school environment for children from ages six to eighteen, many of whom are from single-parent homes and live in public housing. Built in the 1950s at the northwest corner of Franklin Field, the rink was part of the city park system originally designed by Frederick Law Olmsted. The building was an open-air structure covered by long-span bowstring trusses, with a small, brick-enclosed head house containing locker rooms and a basement for mechanical equipment.

Rather than wastefully demolishing the entire hockey rink, the design concept was to weave new elements into the existing structure. Analysis revealed that the ceiling height under the bowstring trusses was too low for the new gymnasium, one of the principal program spaces. However, the ceiling height was appropriate for other uses; consequently, approximately two-thirds of the open-air structure was retained, enclosed, and reoccupied with game rooms, a teen lounge, a library, an art room, and a teaching kitchen. A broad promenade between activity spaces maximizes use of the very wide building footprint and reveals the shed's original trusses and a new skylight. The remaining bays of the old structure were demolished, including the head house, and a new gymnasium and entrance lobby were built on the original foundations.

The gymnasium is a simple rectangular form, its ground-face block presenting the principal facade of the building to the community. A light roof cap of steel trusses and clerestory windows brings in natural light by day and emits a warm, inviting glow at night. The entry zone is transparent and contains a vestibule, front desk, and multipurpose community room. Conceived as a gathering space, the lobby connects the gymnasium to the wide concourse of the activity rooms. Signaling the main public entrance from the street, a colorful steel canopy wraps around a slender steel column topped with a beacon of light. The canopy links the three principal volumes—entry zone, gymnasium, and clubhouse.

Outdoor spaces are integral to the program. At the gymnasium end of the building, a new stage, seating area, and play plaza create a community performance and gathering venue. A restored outdoor swimming pool is immediately visible from the glazed lobby. As the area of the original hockey rink far exceeded indoor program needs, a large covered outdoor play space beyond the activities wing occupies part of the original structure.

The project was developed through a series of public meetings to define the program and to obtain community consensus. The goal was to weave together the community's need for a safe and lively space and an existing unused public structure. The reuse of the existing structure and enclosure constitutes a fundamentally sustainable design endeavor—an environmentally beneficial approach appreciated by the community. Executed with an economy of means on a limited budget, the center is an active and positive neighborhood presence.

Original hockey rink built in the 1950s

Context plan

Axonometric sequence showing
existing building vault and partial
enclosure, vaulted area saved for reuse,
partial enclosure under vault, and new
gymnasium and entry lobby on original
foundations

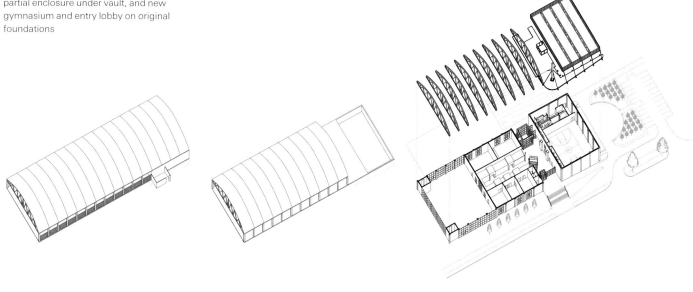

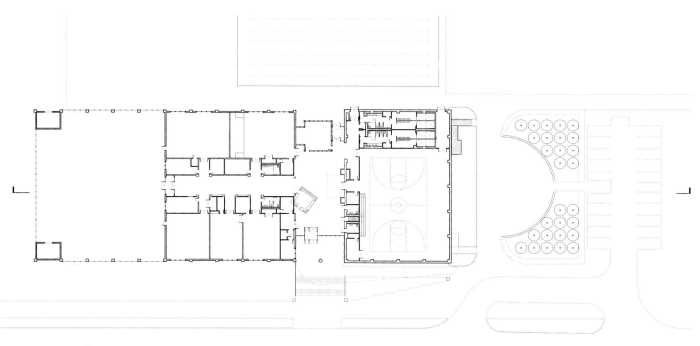

Ground-floor plan ⦵ ⊢————————⊣ 60'

Steel mast topped with a beacon of
light supports sweeping entry canopy

New gymnasium and entry canopy
on foundations of original hockey rink

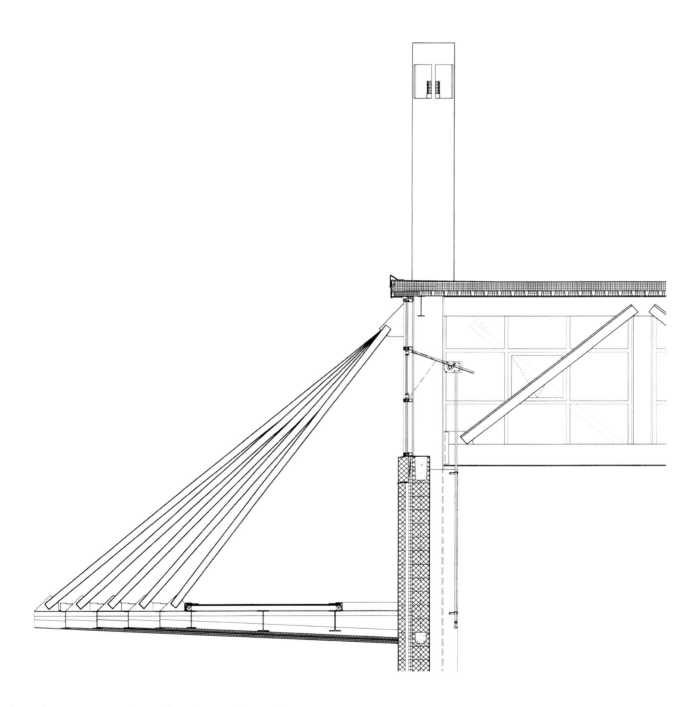

Detail of canopy support and gymnasium clerestory with operable window ⊢————————⊣ 4'

→ Broad promenade lined with portals to activity rooms runs under original vault

→ → Three framed cubes occupy the entry lobby zone, defining vestibule, check-in desk, and meeting room.

↘ Framed glass meeting room provides views through entry lobby to swimming pool

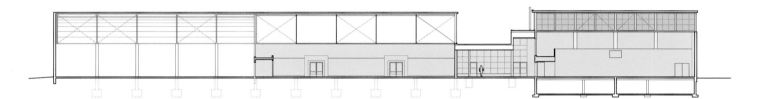

Building section ⌐⎯⎯⎯⌐ 20'

MIT School of Architecture and Planning

Cambridge, Massachusetts, 2004

Originally located within the Massachusetts Institute of Technology's (MIT) prominent "main group" of monumental neoclassic structures built in the early 1900s, the School of Architecture and Planning had steadily outgrown available area. Much of the school's space—organized as three corridors meeting at a central rotunda—had been virtually abandoned when loft space in other buildings became temporarily available. In fact, facilities for the faculty and students were scattered across twelve buildings. The goal of the renovation was to reunite the academic departments, including faculty offices, studio, and review spaces, and to create a coherent identity for the school on three floors within this "main group." The existing fourth floor, the building's attic story, containing most of the studios, had double-loaded corridors that admitted little or no daylight into the interior. There was no visual connection to the studios from the existing rotunda area.

In order to unify the school in one location, a space still undersized for its full program, the design provides locations for reviews, exhibitions, and gatherings in former corridors and passages to accommodate the full program. The new plan creates an ambulatory around the dome, where exhibitions, a cafe, and design reviews enliven the space. Partial views of the dome's coffers strengthen the sense of orientation. The relocation of the double-loaded corridors, from the center to the edge along the solid exterior wall, creates large, windowed studios and one continuous orienting view through exhibition and studio display areas. New and reused skylights along the exterior wall provide an abundance of natural light in the new design-review gallery. By reconfiguring the space around the dome, the renovation unifies the critical mass of studio and review areas, creating a symbolic heart for the school. Double-height space is achieved at the corners of the ambulatory by strategic removal of unused fan rooms, and by replacing former louvered openings with new, tall windows.

Transparency between studios and corridors was a goal to enable display of the studio process to the institute at large. A system of steel-framed glass walls defines the studio walls and doors, creating an interior "urban facade" along the new corridors. A consistent set of framing proportions guides the partitions as they change height and length. Between the gallery and studios, glazed roll-up doors of similar proportion to the fixed walls offer flexibility for students to expand either the studio space or the corridor review space. Moveable partitions within the studios allow students to create shared pin-up spaces and flexible workspaces, which can change as classes change. Plaster walls and the building's massive concrete columns and beams, uncovered and expressed, are woven together with the system of painted, steel-framed glass walls and doors. New skylights illuminate open research space for graduate students located within newly created faculty office suites.

Among the first architecture studio spaces in the country to be fully wired for computers, with power supply and network connections at every student desk, the MIT School of Architecture and Planning anticipates continuous change as more advanced technologies become available. Specialized interactive computer presentation spaces were developed, including the architecture department's Advanced Visualization Theater and the planning department's digital tabletop projection system and adjacent presentation space.

In the third floor departmental office wing, a new exhibition, thesis, and conference space accommodates Frank Stella's 1994 Loohooloo. The ninety-seven-foot-long, three-dimensional, acrylic-on-molded-fiberglass mural completely wraps a new conference room from floor to ceiling.

Based on a master plan developed for the school, phased renovations, each executed in the brief summer months between semesters, were accomplished over a period of several years.

← Steel stairs access a faculty office mezzanine and a graduate studio suite.

Weaving & Embedding

Axonometric, showing studios, galleries,
and offices on several floors

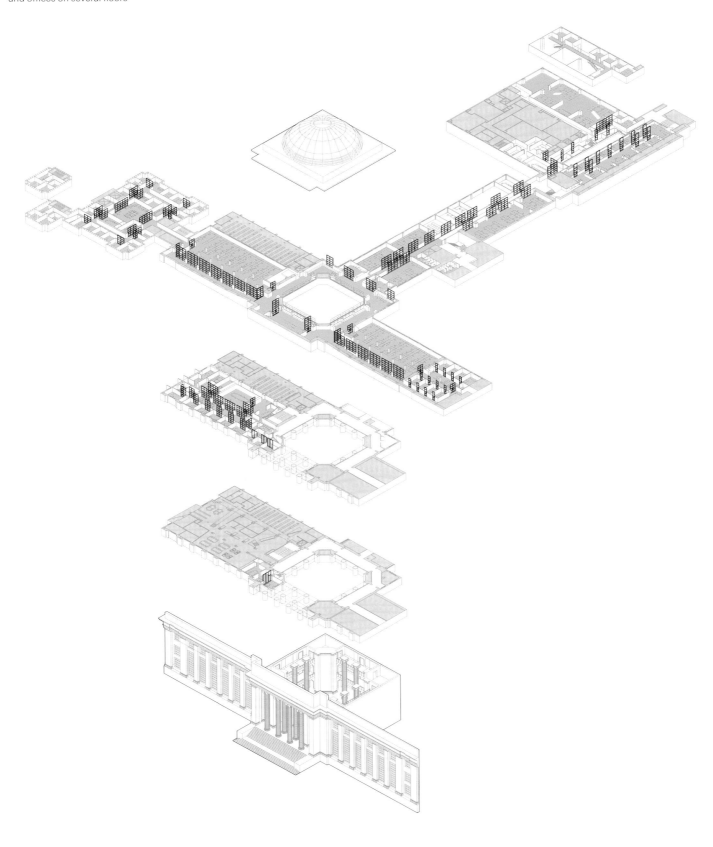

MIT School of Architecture and Planning

Interior elevations of studio steel
glazing system and glazed overhead
garage doors accommodate existing
changes in floor level.

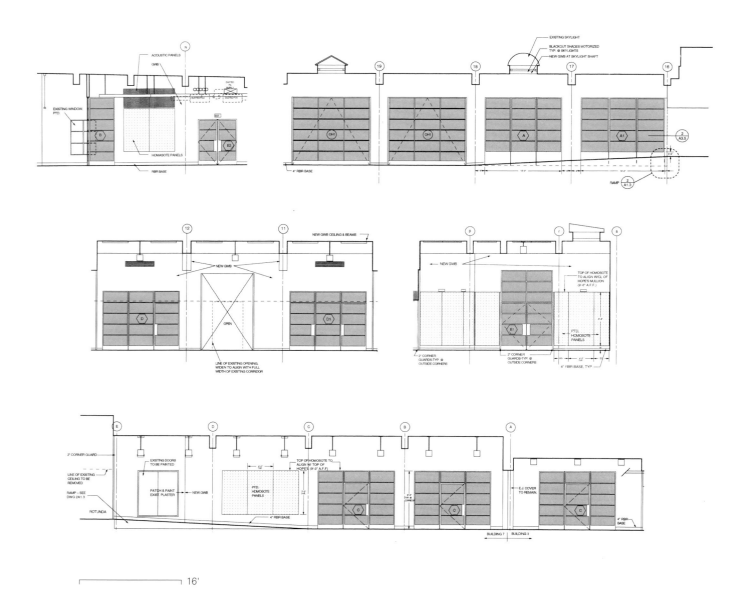

16'

The administrative space outside the Wolk Gallery and most other spaces were studied using computer models and animations, showing lighting ray tracing and all exposed heating, air conditioning, plumbing, and electrical equipment.

The steel glazing system of the studios is repeated at faculty office entries with translucent glass doors and clear glass transoms.

Attic skylights and tall glazed transoms at faculty offices bring light into internal student research space.

Layers of transparency reveal
exhibits on display within the new
Wolk Gallery.

A major three-dimensional mural
by Frank Stella integrated with
conference space provides focus to
the surrounding gallery.

MIT School of Architecture and Planning

Transparency of the studios is a key feature of the newly configured corridors that provide studio review space with pin-up walls, data access, and vertically expanded space.

→ Newly configured studios expand across the former double-loaded corridors to a single-loaded corridor bringing natural light in through glazed overhead garage doors.

Smith College Fitness Center

Northampton, Massachusetts, 2004

The largest undergraduate women's college in the United States, Smith College has demonstrated a long-standing commitment to both the intellectual and physical development of its students. To underscore this priority, the college wished to build a highly visible and inviting fitness center for the use of the entire college community. The facility was envisioned as a campus showcase for recruitment of prospective athletes and as a magnet of social activity, where physical fitness is an integral part of the college experience.

The area available was in the vicinity of two existing athletic buildings—the neoclassical Scott Gymnasium, built in 1920, and the modern Ainsworth Gymnasium, built in 1970—on steeply sloping land at the edge of the campus. Three concepts for siting of the new fitness center offered different opportunities and constraints. A freestanding building adjacent and connected to Scott was the simplest construction option but encroached on a sensitive resi-dential community. A second free-standing option was a stepped and terraced structure on the hillside adjacent to the Ainsworth, which blocked views of and access to Paradise Pond. After close analysis and consul-tation with many campus constituencies, the concept of embedding the project between the existing gymnasia, on top of the former Scott Pool structure, emerged as the most viable option.

The fitness center is conceived as a transparent connector spanning between the two buildings. Its seven thousand square feet of flowing workout space, encased by glass curtain walls and steel, opens to two levels below. The main fitness level is at the main campus entry elevation and connects the first floor of Scott to the third floor of Ainsworth. The level below is a mezzanine with a student lounge and spectator access to the Ainsworth swimming pool. The lowest level contains a lower campus entry, offices, and additional multiuse spaces in the former one-story pool structure. A continuous skylight above the new atrium floods the three levels with natural light, unifying them and providing orientation and focus for the complex space, and a combination of stair, ramp, and bridge links the new structure to the existing elevator for ease of access.

Light steel framing for roof, floors, and skylight minimize loading on existing foundations while heightening the feeling of openness. The silicon-glazed curtain-wall system maximizes the transparency of the window wall, offering views from the fitness center toward the pond and views into the new facility from campus pathways.

Linking three buildings required threading steel columns through eighty-year-old roofs, glazed tile ceilings, and foundations, as well as seismically separating parts of the structure. Mechanical systems for the new building are embedded within the inter-floor space, allowing unob-structed views on the fitness floor. The project improves the energy efficiency of the entire gymnasium complex by reducing the total exterior surface area. Reuse of existing building elements, including foundations, minimized demolition. Locating the fitness center over an existing rooftop between two buildings preserves green space on campus. Careful integration of the new and existing struc-tures solved confusing circulation between the two gyms. The connecting floors create a code-compliant and fully accessible complex.

The new fitness center is a dematerialized light-filled space nested between the brick of Scott and the concrete of Ainsworth; it respects the existing structures by clearly articulating a modern interstitial space with a new purpose and materiality.

← View from main fitness level with bridges at window wall connecting adjacent gymnasia

Campus plan

Model study

Construction sequence showing
framing on top of former swimming
pool, structure spanning between
two existing buildings, and frameless
glazed enclosure

Site plan 🕐 ┌─────────┐ 200'

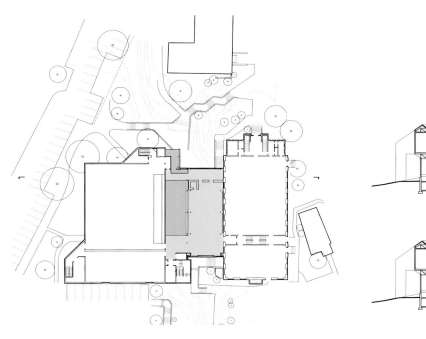

Fitness-level plan ┌─────┐ 60'

Before and after section

→ View from mezzanine level with skylight above bringing light down three stories

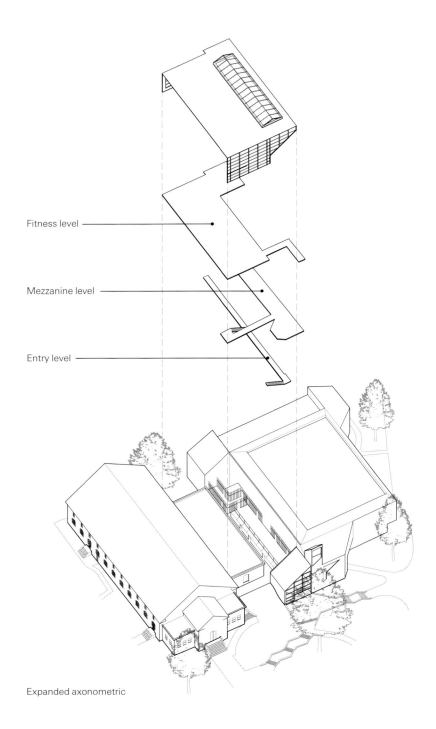

Fitness level

Mezzanine level

Entry level

Expanded axonometric

← ← Supports and bracing for curtain wall on the interior allows exterior to appear frameless

← Detail of curtain wall framing and diagonal steel-rod bracing

↙ View out to the campus from main fitness level

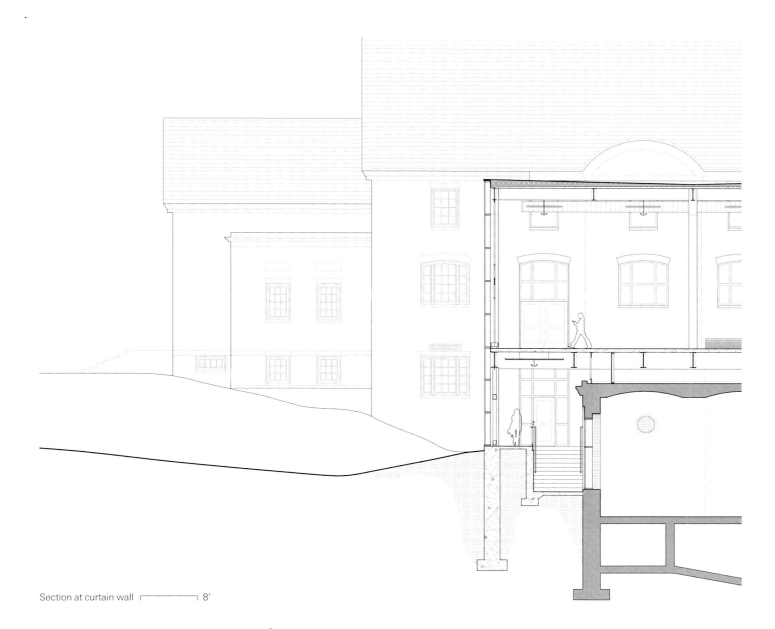

Section at curtain wall ⊢———⊣ 8'

Fitness Center spans between two existing gymnasia over former brick-faced swimming pool.

Harvard University Science Center Expansion

Cambridge, Massachusetts, 2004

When it opened in 1973, Harvard University's Science Center, designed by Josep Lluís Sert, dean of the Graduate School of Design, was the gateway to the extended campus north of Harvard Yard. With its terraced form, light-filled arcades, and rugged palette of textured concrete, it quickly became a modern landmark. By 2000, however, a number of departments housed in the Science Center—History of Science, Statistics, and Computer Services—urgently needed new offices, classrooms, and a visible public exhibition area for the distinguished Collection of Historical Scientific Instruments, then hidden in the basement. Beyond additional space, renovations were critically needed to improve the building's energy efficiency in the arcades, which were lined with single-glazed window walls and leaking skylights. Full building accessibility was also required.

As the existing building filled its entire site, the new space is located in three rooftop additions woven into the body of the building. The main addition, at the East Terrace, is a four-story structure that replaced a one-story wing. This east addition accommodates the Department of the History of Science and the scientific instruments collection, which is prominently located on the ground floor; temporary exhibition space, archives, and the conservation laboratory are on the second floor, and department offices and seminar rooms are located on the top two floors. Computer Services occupies a similar two-story addition at the West Terrace, and the Statistics Department expands at the Central Terrace.

The limitations of the existing structure required the new additions to be lightweight in concept and construction. The additions are minimal; steel-framed glass volumes are set into the sculptural mass of the original building, like crystals embedded in rock. The cast-glass channel cladding is luminous and light—a counterpart to the robust texture of the original precast concrete—and provides a density and rhythm compatible with Sert's building. The glass channels bring light into the interior by day and create a glowing campus presence by night. The development of the East Terrace sets the guidelines for all three additions. The irregular pattern of windows within the glass-channel module reflects the increasing density of occupancy moving up through the building, and echoes a similar informal composition of openings in the original building.

On the interior, spaces for the Department of the History of Science and the Collection of Historical Scientific Instruments are configured as a four-story town house, joined by a new, fully glazed internal stairway to integrate teaching and exhibition activities. Shared lounges and meeting rooms adjacent to the stairway provide an identifiable focus for each floor. Offices along the perimeter wall with translucent corridor partitions, which repeat the vertical panel rhythm, transparency, and translucency of the exterior wall, bring daylight deep into the interior. At the juncture between the new and existing buildings, entries to the first and second floors are joined by a double-height space, as are the third and fourth floors, with access from the main corridor by bridge connections. The ground-floor collection, with its new location on the public level, and second-floor temporary exhibition and archives form a suite of spaces that makes an extraordinary collection available to the public while expanding its use for scholarly scientific research.

← A new four-story East Terrace replaces the original one-story structure. Its compact form wrapped in channel glass contrasts with the material and sculptural forms of the original building while reflecting the proportions and rhythms of its components.
© Alan Karchmer / Esto

The technical challenge of making new additions on top of an existing structure led to several creative solutions. Independent footings-analysis revealed that by reducing soil overburden at some locations, it was possible to develop enough strength in existing foundations to carry the full four-story addition without further foundation work in the existing mechanical basement space. The removed soil area was then available to create a new sloping side-walk and accessible entrance for the entire building complex. In the existing courtyard, which occupies the roof of the building's mechanical room, a new dining terrace and green garden conceals air vents and equipment below.

The new additions substantially improve the original building and meet current energy guidelines. The taut cubic form of the additions maximizes the ratio of interior volume to exterior surface area. The enclosure system is a double-channel glass assembly with a capillary structured trans-lucent insulating layer that transmits light while blocking heat transmission. Replacing leaky single-pane glazing at the courtyard arcades, skylights, and greenhouse cafe with low-E double-glazing and thermal-break aluminum framing reduced energy consumption in the existing building.

Campus plan

Model of East Terrace, Central Terrace, and West Terrace additions

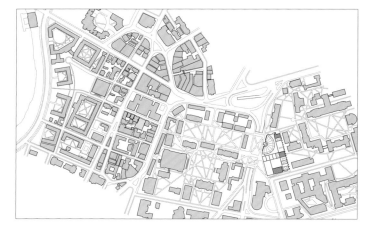

Third-floor plan with East Terrace offices and West Terrace offices and classroom

Ground-floor plan showing the gallery for the Collection of Historical Scientific Instruments entered from main building concourse and opening onto the courtyard

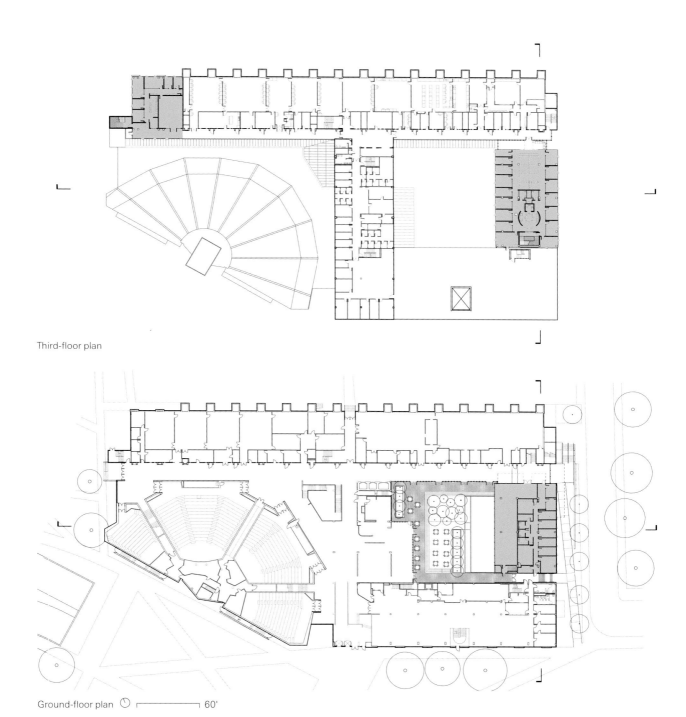

Third-floor plan

Ground-floor plan   60'

Section of four-story East Terrace with gallery, temporary exhibition, and archives on the first and second floors; and History of Science Department offices and classrooms on the third and fourth floors

→ Construction of the four-story East Terrace offered the opportunity to create an accessible pathway for the entire building complex.
© Alan Karchmer / Esto

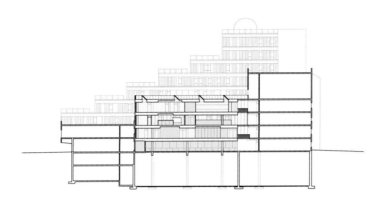

North-south section

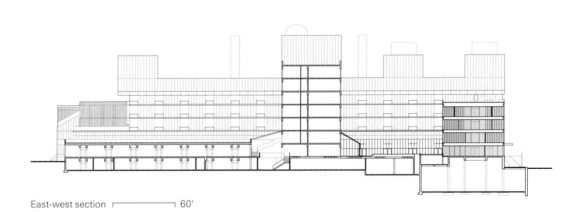

East-west section ⌐————⌐ 60'

Weaving & Embedding

← Detail view of the juncture
between existing precast concrete
and new channel glass envelopes
© Alan Karchmer / Esto

Plan and section details of
channel glass walls, showing
intersections with floor slabs
and interior partitions

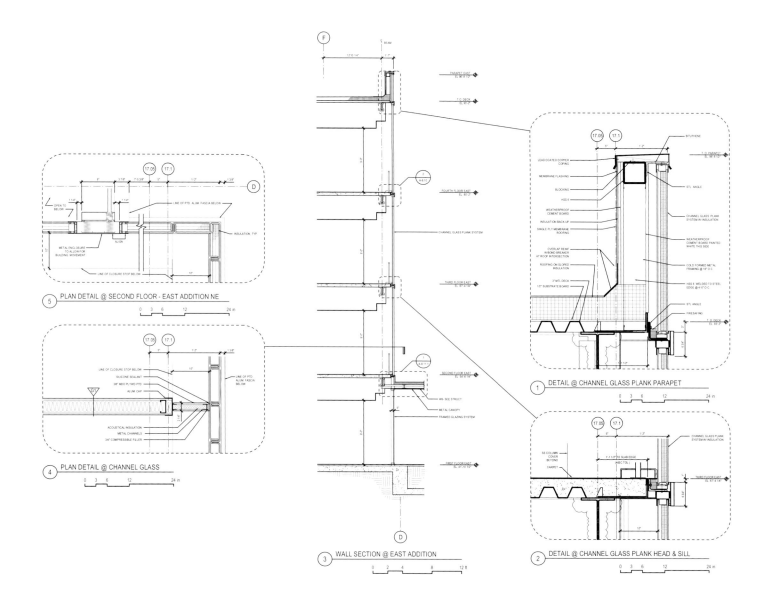

⑤ PLAN DETAIL @ SECOND FLOOR - EAST ADDITION NE

④ PLAN DETAIL @ CHANNEL GLASS

③ WALL SECTION @ EAST ADDITION

① DETAIL @ CHANNEL GLASS PLANK PARAPET

② DETAIL @ CHANNEL GLASS PLANK HEAD & SILL

The expansion frames a newly configured courtyard. The ground is a green roof terrace over the main mechanical space below.

© Alan Karchmer / Esto

→ Translucent channel glass shields the archives from direct light, and clear windows at intervals provide views into the courtyard.

© Alan Karchmer / Esto

← Paired floors join the reception area for the Department of the History of Science with offices and classrooms above.

A flexible temporary exhibition space for student use opens onto adjacent archives and conservation areas.

STITCHING & FITTING

Architecture has a healing function. It can help to mend a torn urban fabric. It can bind together disparate communities. It can begin the repair of social discontinuities by creating physical bridges rather than barriers. Architecture has the ability to be an exceptional center of attraction or a well-mannered participant in a larger conversation. Sometimes it must be both. To fit well, it must suit both its purpose and context with precision, proportion, and good measure.

Stitching together implies an invisible joining of parts. When applied to architecture it means careful consideration of siting, continuity of massing, and positioning and visibility of entries. The mending can add depth and character to the renewed larger fabric. A good fit suggests that architecture conforms in shape and size to its purpose. A good fit is not only about absolute size, but also scale of detail, rhythm, and modulation. Materials—their color, texture, and reflectivity—bind architecture to its physical and social setting.

The following projects, while dramatically different in scale and use, each play a pivotal role in sustaining the continuity of urban fabric, repairing rifts, and supporting the larger framework. At the same time, each project proposes a clear and bold new identity.

Cambridge School of Weston Mugar Center for the Performing Arts

Weston, Massachusetts, 2000

This small independent secondary school wished to underscore its emphasis on the performing arts with the construction of a new performing arts center at the heart of its rural campus in Massachusetts. The need was for a versatile setting for rehearsal and performance of music, drama, and dance education that would become the centerpiece of the campus. A loosely configured quadrangle dotted with trees, crossed with paths, and largely defined by traditional New England two-story buildings was the locus for the new complex. Beyond the relatively flat informal quadrangle, the land slopes steeply down to the school's lower campus and a protected wetlands. The major challenge was to insert a large, new program with a significant theater space into the delicate scale and fabric of the existing campus quadrangle, taking advantage of the steep slope at its edge.

To minimize its sizable mass and ensure that it fits comfortably with its neighbors, the building is carefully inserted into the terrain so that only the topmost of its three floors is visible from the quadrangle. The design consists of three side-by-side volumes embedded in the slope. The principal volume contains a 250-seat experimental theater that can accommodate audiences of up to 300 spectators. The theater takes full advantage of the natural slope, with its entrance and lobby on the quadrangle, and stage and backstage work-areas a full level lower. The upper lobby forms a backdrop for and access to an outdoor stage terrace and natural amphitheater. The second major volume contains the music department with an intimate, seventy-five-seat, multiuse recital and dance hall space, music practice rooms, and director's office at quadrangle level, costume and theater storage at midlevel, and a small black-box theater two full floors below the entry level.

Between the two major elements, and forming the main entry on the quad, is a light-filled, multilevel reception lobby announced by a colorful canopy. A grand stair cascades through the building, following the natural slope of the land. With theater and performance wings to either side, the linear reception lobby functions as a unifying spine, providing access to the lower floors and spectacular views of the landscape beyond. In contrast to the two largely opaque major volumes, the stair zone is glazed at its ends and along its length with a raised clerestory.

With a very limited budget, material choices were critical. Granite curbing forms the curved edge of the outdoor amphitheater and retaining seat-wall. The enclosure of the two exterior solid volumes is painted medium-density overlay plywood with battens. On the interior, continuation of these walls in the public spaces is battened, like the exterior, over acoustic fabric panels and plasterboard. The acoustic metal roof structure is the finish surface through-out most of the building. The floors are polished and colored concrete, and the ceilings are acoustic steel deck supported by exposed steel beams. The walls are painted with accents of color, and doors and cabinetry are made of natural wood.

The key to the theater design was adaptability for dance, plays, assemblies, and classes. The flat-floor stage provides performance flexibility and space for additional seats, as needed. Seating is configured as a curved, shallow amphitheatre to encourage a sense of intimacy. The rear block of seats can be darkened so that a small performance doesn't feel lost in a larger hall. To minimize the height of the theater and the building volume, the trusses spanning the hall also function as catwalks and provide an armature for lighting.

Taken together, the theater, recital hall, black box, and descending interior passage constitute a vibrant and flexible student-oriented venue for performance at every level of the building.

← The entry plinth serves as an informal stage to the small curved amphitheater area.

Site models demonstrated that the major mass of the building would be contained within the downhill slope and away from the main campus quadrangle.

Campus plan

The performing art center is located at the lower end of a gently sloping informal campus quadrangle and has a small connection to an existing dining hall.

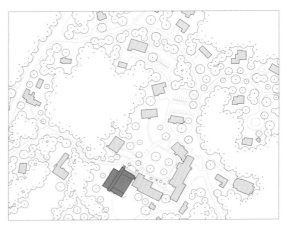

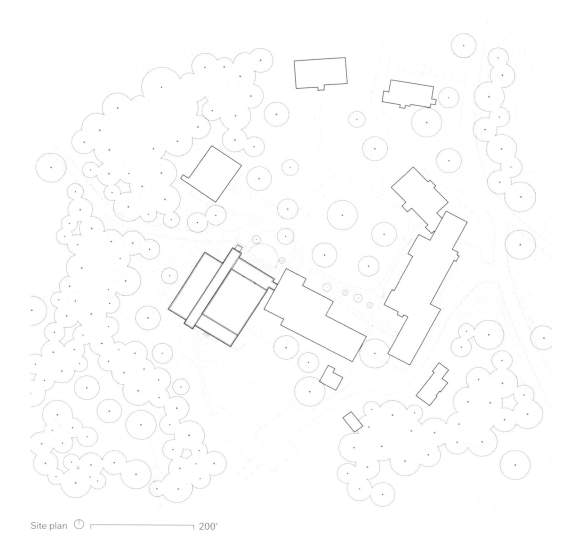

Site plan ① ┌──────────────────┐ 200'

A brightly painted steel canopy welcomes students to the upper level of the complex and to its highly visible theater lobby.

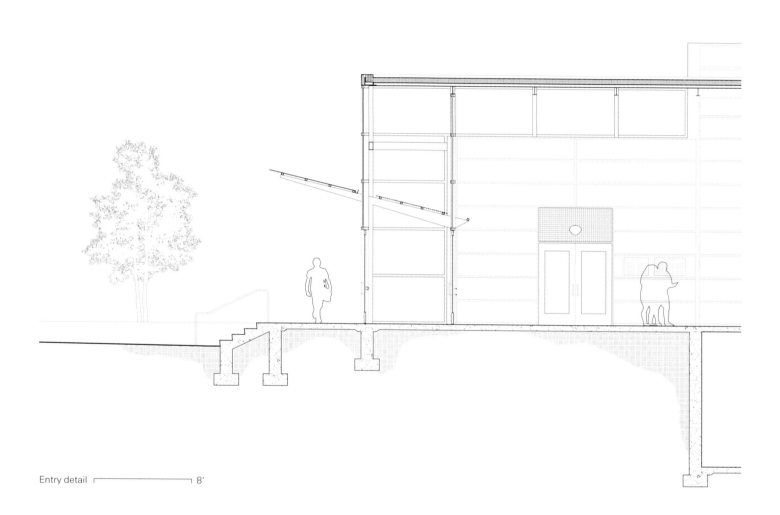

Entry detail ⌐————————⌐ 8'

→ The light-filled vertical lobby with a cascading stair connects three performance levels and terminates with glazed exterior entries at each end.

→ → The board and batten system of the exterior walls continues into the interior of the vertical lobby and accommodates acoustic panels; light colored acoustic metal roof decking and exposed painted steel structure contrast with dark colored polished concrete floors.

↘ The double array of seats in the main theater allow for small audiences to be accommodated in the forward section while the rear section remains darkened.

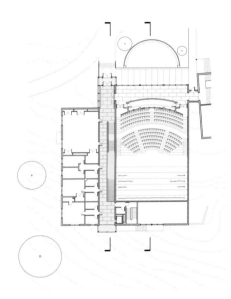

Lobby-level plan

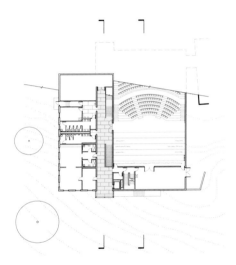

Stage-level plan

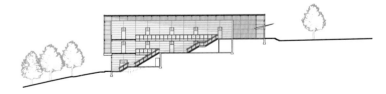

Lobby section

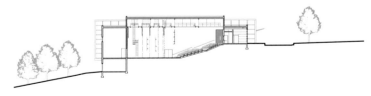

Theater section ⌐———————⌐ 60'

10
12

Harvard University New College Theatre

Cambridge, Massachusetts, 2007

Originally designed in 1887 by Peabody & Stearns, the Hasty Pudding Club building, at the heart of Harvard Square, was home to the venerable social institution for generations of Harvard University undergraduates. Over the years, in addition to the annual Hasty Pudding Show, the club has also presented its famous Man and Woman of the Year Awards. Initially, the building contained clubrooms on two floors at the front of the building and a ballroom with a raised stage at the back. In 1910, the rear portion of the building was rebuilt and enlarged with a shallow sloped theater on the ground floor and dining room above.

Despite its popularity, the private club was unable to maintain the building, and it fell into serious disrepair. Harvard University acquired the building with the intention of transforming it into a fully equipped, professional-quality, 272-seat theater, with rehearsal and support spaces, for use by undergraduates. While Hasty Pudding Theatricals continues to present its annual musical production in the new theater, the revitalized building is available to all student dramatic and musical groups as well as many other Harvard-affiliated groups for productions and performances open to the public, signaling a new era of innovation for the performing arts at Harvard.

Because both the university and the Cambridge community wanted to preserve the building's historic presence, the original front of the 1887 brick structure, its entry porches, and principal spaces were retained and restored for lobby and multipurpose use. The rear structure was demolished to make way for a new six-story theater complex, which fills the midblock site. In order to accommodate the full theater program while maintaining the scale of the neighborhood, the addition has three stories below grade and three above, nearly doubling the original building's size. New and old structures are stitched seamlessly together. From the street, the nineteenth-century structure appears virtually unaltered, revealing its new identity through glimpses of the glass- and zinc-clad volumes. By transforming the adjacent alley into a sloped sidewalk and through-block pathway to the side lobby, the inaccessibility of the historic entry, with its porch and stairs, was eliminated.

← Entrances at original porch and at ramped alleyway lead to lobby and main stage as well as upper rehearsal and performance areas.

© Alan Karchmer / Esto

Inside, the new side lobby joins the restored porches and front rooms to create waiting and reception space for the theater. A state-of-the-art theater with a full range of support spaces has been snugly fit into a space that formerly housed the dilapidated two-story rear wing. Entering the theater offers a dramatic contrast between old and new. The new space is a generous three-story volume, stepping down a full floor to the stage in a steep rake that gives every seat an unencumbered view. Above the audience chamber, a big, airy rehearsal room, separated acoustically from the performances below, doubles as a black box theater. Below the main stage are two floors containing dressing rooms, props storage, and mechanical space.

Just as the new theater complex is tucked within the block, the audience chamber is similarly inserted into the fabric of the building. As a teaching theater for nonprofessional performers, the space is configured to create an intimate relationship between audience members and actors. A broad cross aisle divides the audience chamber into a small front section and larger rear section, allowing modestly sized performances to feel comfortable in the space. Because the site is extremely confined, there is only space for a seating gallery on one side of the theater.

Fitting the new program into the available space behind the original building required many elements to serve double or triple duty. A window in the gallery (with darkening shades), opening onto a mid-block garden, allows the space to be used in the daytime for student meetings. Opposite the gallery, the audience chamber has large panels opening into the theater from the lobby, extending the performance space for speakers and musicians. The full width of the stage, with a proscenium created by curtains when needed, opens directly onto the audience chamber. At the front of the stage a platform lift travels up and down to create a stage extension, move sets and pianos, or to create an orchestra pit.

The richly colored interior concept for the theater space is a crimson volume split by an aubergine entry zone. Deep-red, aniline-dyed plywood paneling and ceiling air diffusers lined with blue LED tubes create a bold environment for student productions. Equipped with a transformable stage, full fly loft, and the capacity for lighting and audiovisual experimentation, the flexible performance space provides both a rich educational experience and a valuable community asset.

Campus plan

Audience chamber
concept model

Original Hasty Pudding Club by
Peabody and Stearns, 1887
Harvard University Archives, call # HUV595 (BP 9)

A tower crane was required to
construct the new building on its
highly constrained site

Detail of juncture between original
building, new zinc-clad stairwell, and
glazed rehearsal room/black box

New and restored lobbies
surround new audience chamber
and stage, tightly fitting
within the block.

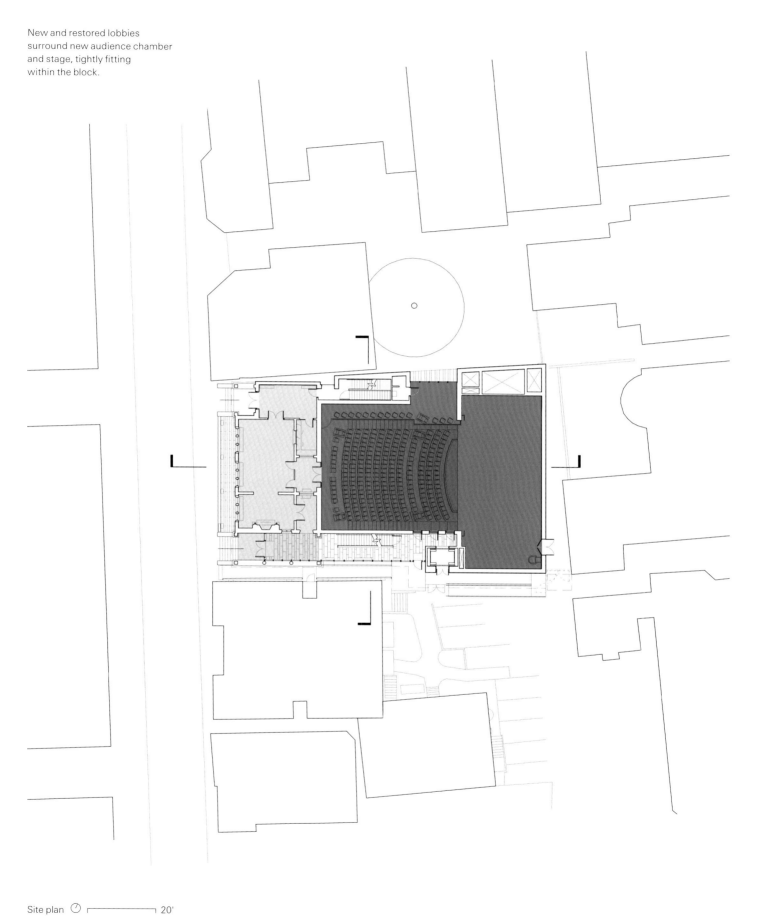

Site plan 🕐 ⌐————————⌐ 20'

Restored front rooms and porches
of original Hasty Pudding Club with
new theater complex behind
© Alan Karchmer / Esto

→ Restored original front lobby
© Alan Karchmer / Esto

Section showing audience chamber
with space for only one gallery on
its narrow site

Section showing restored original
building front and new theater
and stage with rehearsal/black box
above and theatre support and
mechanical space below

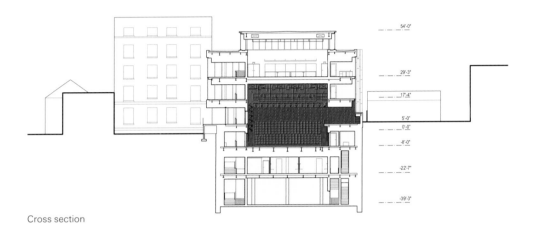

Cross section

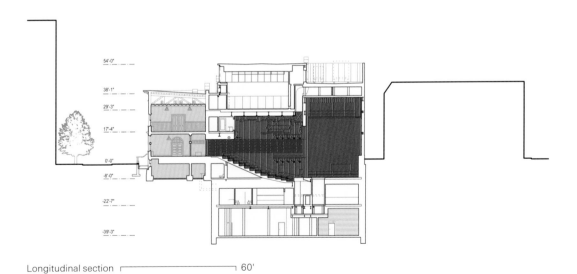

Longitudinal section ⌐⎯⎯⎯⎯⎯⎯⎯⎯⌐ 60'

The curved seating bank of the audience chamber is divided by a cross aisle to create a lower section of seats for small presentations. A window onto a mid-block garden at the gallery can be darkened for performances.

© Alan Karchmer / Esto

The audience chamber with gallery on one side is lined with aniline-dyed wood wall panels, and capped by a darkened ceiling, catwalk zone, and LED illuminated diffusers.

Digital study model of audience chamber

Detail of deeply colored walls and seating

→ View of projection booth and lighting bank at rear of theatre

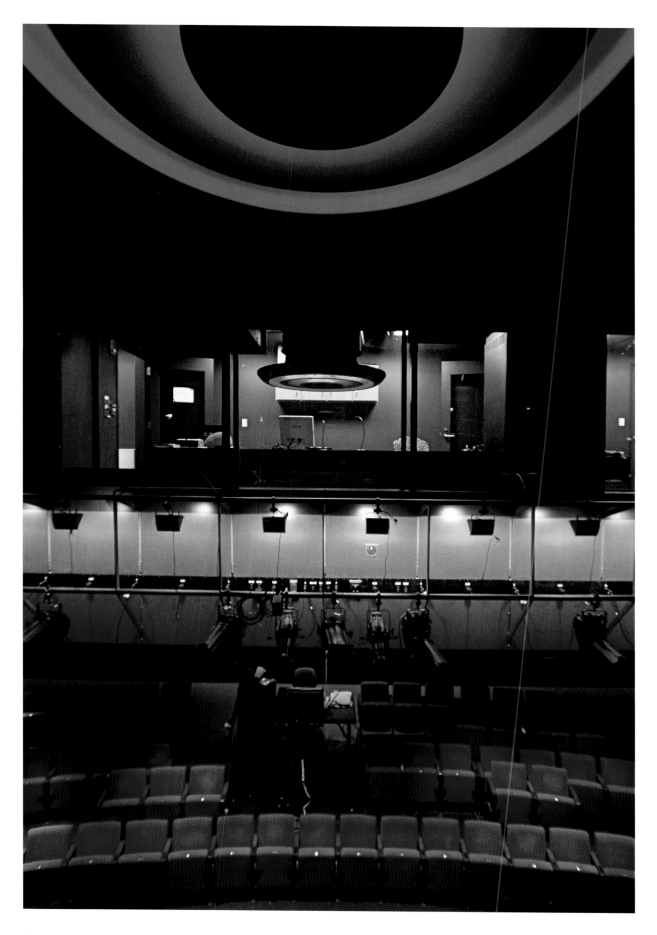

Harvard University New College Theatre

Harvard University Library Services Building

Cambridge, Massachusetts, 2006

Previously dispersed throughout the campus, Harvard University Library Services required centralized support space for its library system, including the Office for Information Systems and the Weissman Preservation Center for rare books. The designated site for the Harvard University Library Services Building fronts on Mount Auburn Street, in Cambridge's historic Harvard Square area, one of the first streets of the original village. Three- to six-story freestanding buildings of varied rooflines, materials (brick, wood, stone), and styles surround the small parcel. Community groups placed a high priority on creating a building of suitable scale with an attractive pedestrian environment, and on retail uses at street level. The challenge required maximizing useable area while limiting building height.

Massing studies began with a careful analysis of the heights, materials, and rhythm of buildings and the open spaces between them along Mount Auburn Street. The volume of the new building was determined by limiting the roof height to the ridges of nearby buildings and setting back from the side property line to establish consistent intervals along the street. The setback created space for a new through-block pathway paved in brick and lined with wood fencing and trees, an uncommon landscape amenity in this densely built part of Harvard Square.

The new building is a compact volume with four stories above grade and two stories below. Along the sidewalk, ground-floor retail space with display windows and a separate entry protected by a canopy enliven the pedestrian experience. The entrance to the Library Services Building at the corner leads to a reception and lounge running the length of the through-block path. At the top floor, sculptural skylights bring daylight into the preservation laboratory and create a crown for the building. The second and third floors contain Information Systems offices.

Concrete flat slab construction minimizes the overall building height. The plan is laid out in a loose nine-square grid, adapted to the irregular outline of the site. The building envelope is composed of a glass window wall facing active Mount Auburn Street on the north side and a terra-cotta rain-screen wall with protected openings at mid-block on the east, south, and west sides. The modest floor plate of approximately four thousand square feet demanded a minimal core, which was achieved by using scissor stairs. Carefully detailed formwork for the exposed ceiling slab allows a full nine feet of ceiling height. Random-width board-formed concrete gives the core an intensely tactile quality.

With its window wall facing Mount Auburn Street, the building projects an image of openness to the public. Its glass and concrete profile is carefully scaled and proportioned to respond to the grain of surrounding buildings. The facade is divided into three bays: a projected bay at the entry to the offices marks the corner of the building and the pathway.

The concept of the building is guided by environmental considerations: the building envelope is open to the north for maximum daylight, while masonry construction with smaller, shaded openings limits heat gain from the remaining sides. Geothermal wells and heat pumps provide heating and cooling and eliminate the need for rooftop mechanical equipment. A storm-water retention system and reduced water and energy consumption measures contributed to the project's LEED Gold certification from the U.S. Green Building Council.

← A slim concrete structure and two underground floors allow the new building to nestle into its neighborhood context at a modest height, while achieving the program areas needed.

Campus plan

The entry bay cantilevers forward
to the street and invites the public
to enter the passage alongside the
building beyond.

→ Street elevation study, massing,
materials, and spacing informs
the new building's scale and
proportions.

Ground-floor plan ◐ ⌐─────┐ 50'

Ground-floor plan ◐ ⌐─────────┐ 20'

Study models explore changes in the facade articulation and skylight configuration.

→ Section perspective indicating north-facing glazing, skylights, and geothermal wells

↘ Entry-projected volume and extended canopy shelter and enliven ground-level retail-oriented street life.

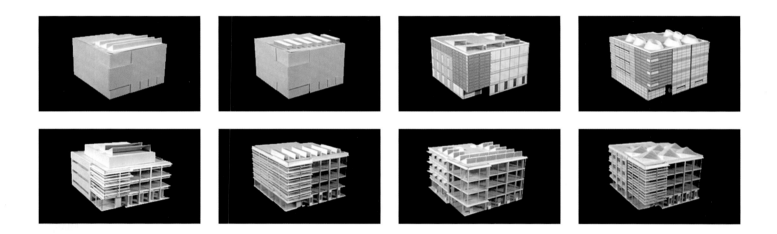

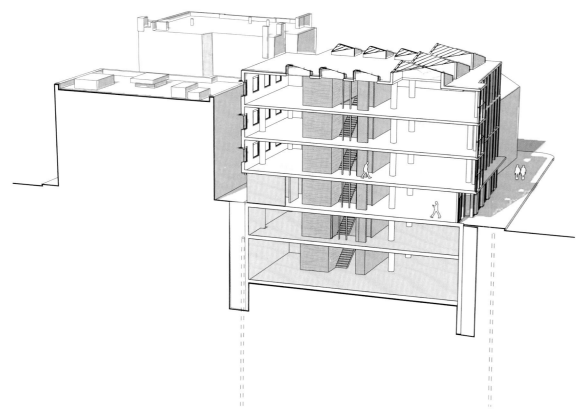

A public through-block passage provides outlooks and views despite the tight urban site.

The terra-cotta rain screen system enclosing the upper floors on the inner-block facades relates to the traditional masonry of the neighboring buildings.

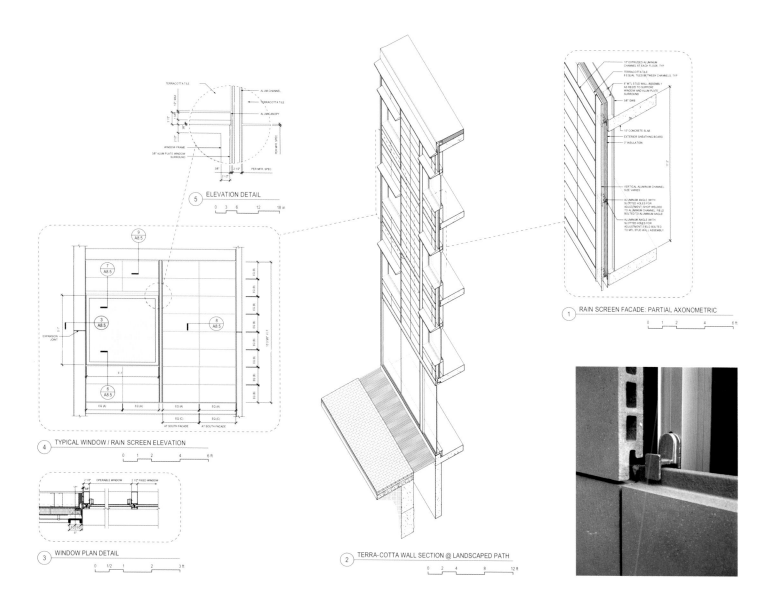

ELEVATION DETAIL

5   0   3   6   12   18 in

4   TYPICAL WINDOW / RAIN SCREEN ELEVATION

0   1   2   4   6 ft

3   WINDOW PLAN DETAIL

0   1/2   1   2   3 ft

1   RAIN SCREEN FACADE: PARTIAL AXONOMETRIC

0   1   2   4   6 ft

2   TERRA-COTTA WALL SECTION @ LANDSCAPED PATH

0   2   4   8   12 ft

Board-formed concrete of
variable widths defines the
scissor stairs.

→ North-facing skylights with
automatic louvers provide light
needed for delicate book and
map restoration.

Ground-floor vitrines display
rare and retail books, while library
book conservation activity is
visible above.

A tall precast concrete entry tower
contrasts with the silvery metal
enclosure and monumental screened
window of the great hall.

U.S. District Courthouse

Orlando, Florida, 2007

As part of its Design Excellence Program, the U.S. General Services Administration planned a large courthouse to accommodate expanded services provided by the Middle District of Florida. Located adjacent to an existing 1970s federal building and courthouse, the new courthouse provides fifteen courtrooms, space for supporting departments, secure U.S. Marshals Service facilities, and parking for 220 cars.

The site for the new courthouse is in downtown Orlando, a city that flourished first as a locus for the citrus industry and later as a center of aviation (and the home of Cape Canaveral) and a tourist destination. An elevated highway and an on-grade railroad line, running north–south, divide the city. The east side is relatively prosperous, with a well-defined commercial center and gracious residential areas dotted with lakes. The oldest buildings of this area date to the early twentieth century. The Post Office and Federal Building, built in 1941, is a particularly interesting example, combining elements of Federal, Spanish Mission, and Italian Rationalism. In contrast, the west side of the city contains struggling residential neighborhoods, some of which have been cleared and residents relocated to create a government center, including the courthouse project parcel.

The site for the new courthouse encompasses a full block immediately adjacent to the elevated highway that divides the east and west sides of the city. Central Boulevard, the principal east–west connecting street, forms its southern boundary. The 1970s federal building—a six-story, precast-concrete structure—occupies the northeast corner of the block.

Because the courthouse would be the largest new construction in the downtown area in several years, its size and prominence offered a significant opportunity to mend the damaged urban fabric. Fitting a large civic structure into a marginalized mixed-use community, including light industry, residential areas, and other governmental uses, posed a further challenge. The design response was to site the new courthouse and a parking structure along the southern edge of the block to define Central Boulevard and to strengthen the east–west connections within Orlando. The newly established street wall can be seen from the east side of the city beyond the elevated highway.

The size of the courthouse in its mixed-scale context was the subject of careful study. An early option proposed a long, low building of three stories lining Central Boulevard. In this approach, surface parking left little space for a public garden, which would benefit the adjacent neighborhood. The final version is a taller, more compact design, making space for a parking structure to complete the facade along Central Boulevard. It also left ample space at the interior of the block for a public garden. Articulating the public lobby as a five-story volume and the administrative wing as a two-story volume surrounding the body of the building mitigates the height of the six-story structure. A tower recalling the 1941 Post Office and Federal Building marks the entrance at the southwest corner of the building.

Together, the new courthouse, the parking structure, and the existing 1970s Federal Building create a public garden at the interior of the block. A connecting passageway between the three structures contains a small cafe overlooking the park. The park, which is slightly raised and fenced to create a secure perimeter, has shade trees, benches, and a central lower lawn at the original grade of the site so that a group of existing mature trees could be retained.

The courthouse building is conceived as an overlapping series of layers, from public to private. Along Central Boulevard, the historic east–west corridor of Orlando, a public atrium of five stories with a screened window wall opens to the community. Each floor of the six-story middle zone has four courtrooms overlooking either the atrium, or the roof terrace and the city beyond.

The palette of exterior materials underscores the programmatic layering and modulates the scale of the project. The body of the building and tower are precast concrete; the atrium, entry canopy, roof terrace canopy, and lower administration wing are clad in a light metal paneling. At the atrium window wall facing Central Boulevard, a fine-grain metal sunscreen creates an additional layer. On the remaining three sides, irregular window patterns and precast panel joints introduce a subtle counterpoint to the rigor of the overall concept.

The public entrance to the new courthouse begins at the tower and opens directly onto the light-filled atrium, which is shaded on its south side by a sunscreen composed of closely spaced perforated metal horizontal louvers admitting a dappled light. Administrative departments are visible and accessible. Facing the entry at the end of the atrium is the two-story, limestone-clad Jury Assembly suite, with a public stair rising to lobby terraces above. The terrace at the third-floor level provides a generous waiting area for the Special Proceedings Courtroom. The focus of the public space is a monumental stained-glass window created by the artist Al Held for the end wall of the atrium above the third-floor terrace.

A fundamental environmental goal of the design is to provide natural light in each of the fifteen courtrooms. Judges' private chambers are configured as pavilions around "light terraces," which allow daylight to enter the courtrooms behind the bench at alcoves lined in a local coquina stone.

With its public spaces looking outward to the city, and its private spaces looking inward to the garden, the courthouse fulfills both its civic purpose and its mission to provide secure and efficient judicial services. The unified courts campus reestablishes the city block, stitches together a divided urban landscape, and provides a modern landmark for Orlando.

Urban context plan

Fronting on Central Boulevard, the new courthouse reinforces the connection with downtown Orlando beyond the elevated highway.
© Peter Aaron / Esto

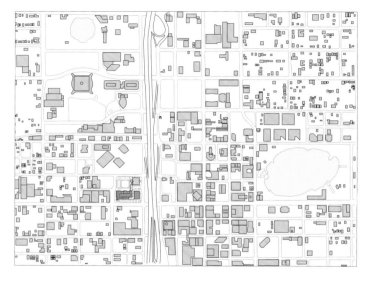

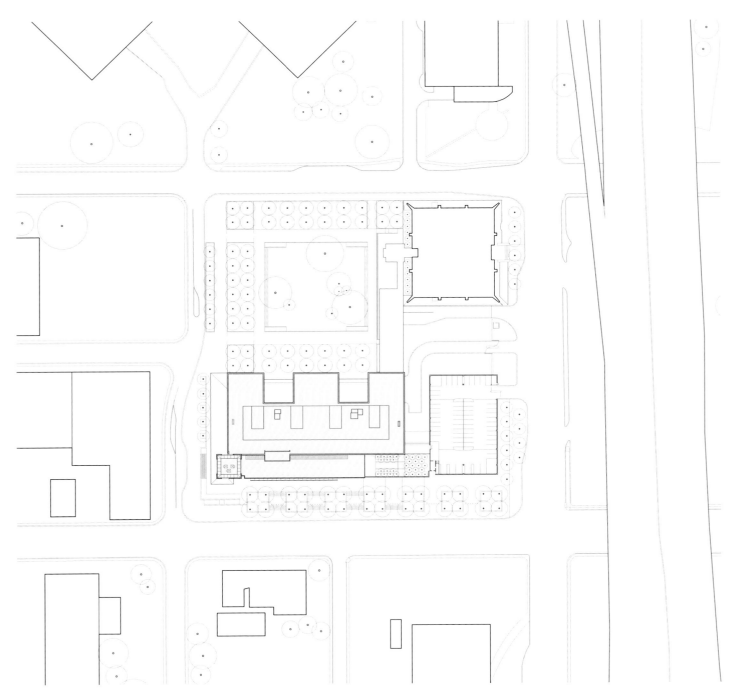

Site plan ⊕ ⌐————⌐ 100'

The courts complex includes a new public park, the new courthouse, a secure garage structure, and the 1970's Federal Building, all connected via secure walkways.

© Peter Aaron / Esto

Study of tower, great hall with window wall, and elevated terrace

Study of prior three-story scheme with great hall, porch, and articulated ceremonial courtroom

The neighborhood approach from a new public park shelters visitors under a long metal canopy.
© Peter Aaron / Esto

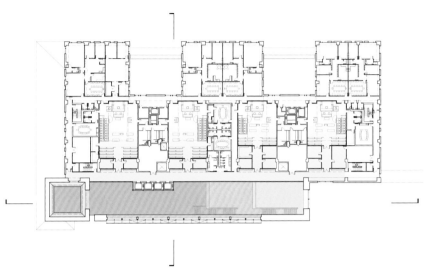

Typical courtroom-floor plan

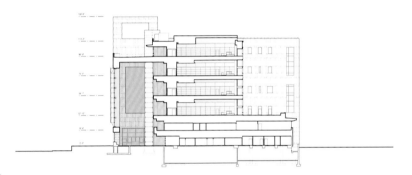

Cross section

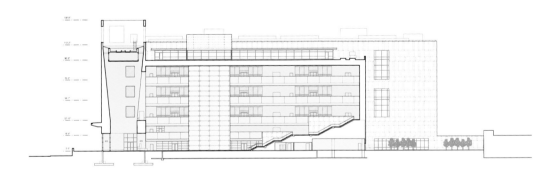

Entry tower and Great Hall section ⊢⸺⸺⸺⸺⊣ 60'

← The great hall, suffused with filtered light from the sun screened window wall, leads to the jury assembly suite, upper waiting terraces, and culminates in a large stained glass window by the artist Al Held.

A view from the waiting terraces looks back to the entry tower, glass elevator shaft, and courtroom entries.

→ Finely calibrated sun screening provides a dappled light in the great hall.

© Peter Aaron / Esto

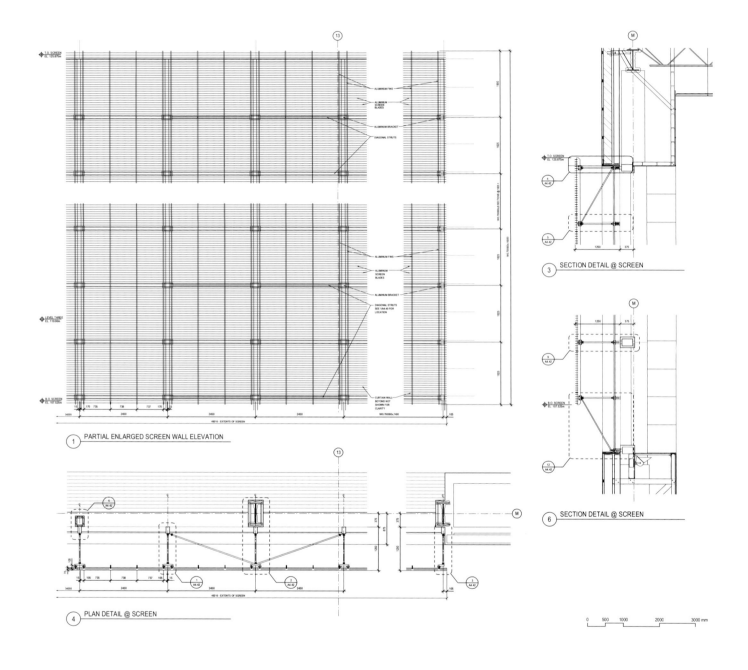

1 PARTIAL ENLARGED SCREEN WALL ELEVATION

4 PLAN DETAIL @ SCREEN

3 SECTION DETAIL @ SCREEN

6 SECTION DETAIL @ SCREEN

← Natural light from the entry
tower skylight illuminates the lobby
and security area below.

© Peter Aaron / Esto

An accessible walled garden
enhances the jury assembly area.

© Peter Aaron / Esto

Above the judge's bench, light enters across a private corridor from north light terraces. At the public entry, light enters across the public hall from the south.

Borrowed daylight from the light terraces washes the front of the courtroom, illuminating a panel of local coquina stone behind the judge.
© Peter Aaron / Esto

→ Cherry wood paneling and custom seating in the courtrooms is brightened by borrowed light from corridors overlooking the great hall.
© Peter Aaron / Esto

→ → Sunlight through the stained glass windows projects unexpected splashes of color on walls and floor.
© Peter Aaron / Esto

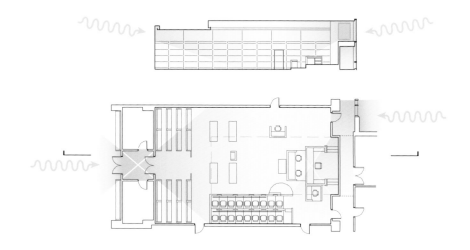

IN CONVER—
—SATION

Composite Conditions, Tectonic Exploration, Human Measure

Leers Weinzapfel Associates is a group of builders. They anchor their projects to site and context not simply through formal expression, but through a deep investigation of constituencies, histories, cultures, programs, and materials.

When Andrea Leers and Jane Weinzapfel established the firm in 1982 they set an unambiguous goal: create bold and refined work that has a positive public impact. Much has changed in the intervening years, from the size of the staff to the diversity of its portfolio, but the design philosophy remains true to the founding partners' commitment to a humanistic architecture. Their sensibility draws on important lessons from early influences, especially the work of Louis Kahn, and from Leers's ongoing research and role as an educator in Japan.

Their practice is characterized by its ability to resolve unusually complex design challenges, whether engaging and expanding existing infrastructure, creating a site where none exists, or extracting opportunities from highly constrained conditions. The collaborative environment of the office and the ability to respond to multiple client constituencies further distinguishes the firm's working method.

The architects' predilection for dynamic buildings, expressive detailing, and tough materials has long defined the firm's work. Consideration of tectonic issues, and the craft of building, is essential to their process.

Nearly three decades on, Leers and Weinzapfel, along with principals Joe Pryse and Josiah Stevenson, reflect on the essential issues and ideas that guide the firm's interventions within the public realm of the city and the academic community of the campus.

Composite Conditions

ABBY BUSSEL: *Your practice is known for tackling projects characterized by complex site conditions. How do you, for example, invent a site where none exists?*

Operation Control Center, model at 1/32" = 1'- 0"

ANDREA LEERS: In tight urban or campus settings there often is no site, or certainly no unencumbered site, so we've had some cases where the only option was to make vertical additions, like the Operations Control Center (OCC) or Harvard Science Center (HSC). Some sites have been constrained by infrastructure or by their shape, as was the case at the University of Pennsylvania. Others are less than obvious. At the Smith Fitness Center, for example, the best site was tucked in between and on top of existing structures.

JOSIAH STEVENSON: The Smith College project was especially interesting because we interviewed for it before a site had been selected. The college offered us a parking lot and a steeply sloped parcel, among others, but there were problems with each location. In the end, we proposed a bridge building that spanned between two existing gymnasiums. Although it was somewhat more expensive to thread a structure through existing foundations, the design enhanced the complex as a whole, creating a lively connection and a place to see and be seen. The infill made the adjacent buildings accessible and, by actually decreasing the surface area, more energy efficient.

LEERS: The Pennsylvania Chiller Plant had a site, but it was a parcel encumbered by its irregular shape, which was defined by the edge of a river, roadways, and a rail line. The solution was to create an elliptical form for the building that most easily adjusted to the curve of the river and allowed the athletic field to be located with the optimal orientation for play.

JANE WEINZAPFEL: Issues such as tough soils and fixed underground utility lines shape the location and cost of a building, too. In urban settings there are also view corridors to address concerns about porosity and pedestrian movement through the site, so the investigation is larger than just the ground plane or building.

AB: *Can you speak to site sensitivities in terms of history and community?*

LEERS: At the University of Cincinnati, our building displaced a vital campus pathway and gathering space. A bridge used as a place of student demonstrations was to be demolished to make way for a new common and a new building. Our brief was to create a building, the University Pavilion, for the campus as a whole. Our obligation was to insert a path through the building, as well as one parallel to it on the outside of the building, which together would reimagine the campus's larger social agenda.

AB: *How do you address the accretions of time when invited to renovate or expand an existing building or group of buildings?*

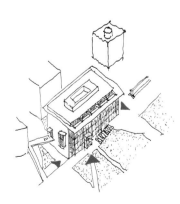

University of Cincinnati Pavilion, entry diagram

WEINZAPFEL: We prioritize the identification of social capital that's invested in an existing building or complex, and analyze its texture and scale and what makes it important to its community. The same effort is applied to the investigation of surrounding buildings, topography

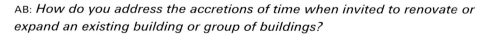

and pathways to take stock of consistencies or inconsistencies represented by different scales, different textures, and different materials.

LEERS: The question of building over time is fundamental to the way we begin thinking about each new project. We always begin by assuming that cities and campuses are living entities. They're not fixed. And we have an obligation to contribute in our time and our voice, while being part of an evolving fabric. The sense of expressing our moment is always foremost in our minds.

JOE PRYSE: We might take cues from the existing buildings, but we never mimic what's there.

AB: *Your studio views its work as part of an ensemble, as part of a context of existing buildings, pedestrian and vehicular routes, and competing— or complementary—agendas. How do you develop an appropriate dialogue with other buildings in the ensemble?*

LEERS: We begin with a close reading of the context. We look carefully at what's there and why it's there, what its really good parts are, what are less compelling parts, and then determine how our work both extends that context and is distinct from it. We look to massing, material, and, of course, to program.

Massachusetts General Hospital Museum and Campus, model at 1/32" = 1'- 0"

WEINZAPFEL: And we look well beyond the site. When we look at where we are positioning a new building, one question is: Does a hierarchy exist within the block, or is it missing? In some cases, for example on a college campus where there are several important voices and we are adding another equally strong voice, the result is akin to a quartet, in which several voices are heard individually but together they add up to a coherent ensemble.

LEERS: Our approach to building in the ensemble is aligned with the attitudes that prevail in Europe. In this country, especially in New England, a sentimental view of our past prevails, and it influences new additions. Our attitude tends to follow in the vein of European urbanism in which the past is valued but not at the expense of envisioning the future.

AB: *When confronting composite conditions—complex sites and contexts— what is the role of the client and other constituencies?*

WEINZAPFEL: There is the client who is building the project and there is the local neighborhood that has a range of voices, and together they become a kind of composite client. The client who is leading the building initiative knows the goals for the project acutely and conveys how these contribute to the larger vision of the institution, as with the wish for transparency at the MIT School of Architecture and Planning. In most of our projects an active user group can further these goals by providing the nuanced particulars of the program, as was the case at the Ohio State University World Media and Culture Center (2005).

Together with the client, we also project the interests of the absent or future users who may not have a place at the table: the patrons of the subway station, the visitors to the courthouse, the students who will be the major

Jackson Square Youth Development Center, digital animation

users of a classroom building. At the Harvard University Library Services building, for example, neighbors were very involved in how the project was going to work for the community.

LEERS: The project was developed after a prior scheme conceived by another architect failed to gain the approval of the Cambridge Historical Commission. The Commissioners never said that the library sciences project needed to be a traditional building. They were concerned with scale, height, and the visibility of rooftop mechanical equipment. We proposed a distinctly modern structure with a glass wall to the north that was carefully scaled to the street. In the end, the community called it a jewel box. They felt that the issues they cared about had been addressed, even though the building is quite different from the immediate fabric. It is not brick. It is not historic in massing or detail.

The genesis of an idea can come from many voices. Being able to interpret them in built form is part of what propels us forward when we're thinking about the design.

Taunton Courthouse, existing structure and new construction

STEVENSON: But standing apart from the ensemble is not always the appropriate response. In fact, the challenges are greater when we're asked to design a building that doesn't stand out.

For example, our new courthouse in Taunton, Massachusetts, is adjacent to a wonderful old Richardsonian courthouse. The program requires a building many times the size of the existing structure and the challenge is not to overwhelm the iconic courthouse.

WEINZAPFEL: We're providing a contemporary partner.

STEVENSON: Right. We intend to create a partnership, not overwhelm the older courthouse and tower structure. We created a building similar in height and material with a bold glass tower in counterpoint to the massive stone.

LEERS: The University of North Carolina, a campus that sees itself in the tradition of the University of Virginia and has a very conservative architectural viewpoint, invited our office to design an international studies center. Some trustees of the school were very enthusiastic about the idea that this building should be forward looking, but others were more apprehensive. A group of trustees traveled to Harvard to look at the richness and variety of its architecture. We stood with them on a spot where H. H. Richardson's Sever Hall can be seen across the street from Le Corbusier's Carpenter Center, with two or three other notable works in close proximity. We talked about how there's a conversation between the old and the new. The tour was tremendously persuasive. They understood that it was possible to design a forward-looking building in a way that would be part of their campus's existing fabric. And that's what we did.

Tectonic Exploration

AB: *Leers Weinzapfel Associates conducts research and pursues innovation through the design process, not through theoretical exploration. How does this contribute to the firm's use of materials?*

LEERS: We are people who love making buildings. We're all motivated at heart by the love of building, the love of craft, of seeing things realized, not just as propositions. I think that's where we derive our pleasure and...

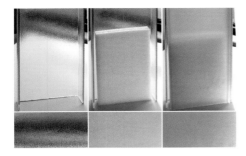

Harvard Science Center, glass channels: single channel, channel with insulation, insulated double channel

Milton Academy Ayer Observatory

PRYSE: ...our satisfaction. Conducting research on materials for a specific project makes it more relevant. Often we look for a new material that will meet the client's goals. We research it with a purpose.

STEVENSON: Because our forms tend to be fairly simple in design, the importance of our materials investigation is elevated.

PRYSE: How materials come together, how they are joined and intersect at corners, is critical for us.

LEERS: We begin each commission like a research project in terms of materials. There's the choice of material, which has to do with responding to the place and to its purpose, and then there are the issues of materials choices, which respond to the wider use of resources, and then all of that is tailored to each situation. Here is where the idea of made to measure is evident. For example, our chiller-plant projects at the University of Pennsylvania and Princeton University have two very different materialities. In Pennsylvania, the plant is wrapped in a light screen wall to accommodate the odd shape of the site and its visibility at the campus gateway. At Princeton, stone was chosen to echo the campus's defining character.

STEVENSON: There is a tendency in the profession to use materials in a trendy way, but we really try to concentrate on their highest and best use. Our buildings act as research projects that create the culture of our studio. There was a point where, for instance, glass planks were in fashion for a little while, and we've used glass planks, most notably at the Harvard University Science Center, and that was really the correct use of that material. The existing building by Sert is a precast concrete plank veneer and we chose to make the additions a lighter glass plank veneer. It was the right use for that material in that building.

WEINZAPFEL: We used perforated, stainless steel panels in the chiller plant at the University of Pennsylvania because we had earlier researched, tested, and specified them for a commuter-rail project as durable windscreens that also provided a measure of visibility necessary for public safety. For the chiller-plant screen we tested the lighting with a horizontal full-size mockup in a parking lot at night. And we test new or alternative materials to failure when appropriate.

STEVENSON: Our research also addresses budget issues. We used a weather-resistant medium-density overlay plywood on the Ayer Observatory (1992) at Milton Academy and we applied that experience to the Cambridge School of Weston. The school's performing arts building is much bigger than the observatory and has different proportions, but our cladding choice was a very cost-effective solution that is aging well.

PRYSE: Sustainability influences our selection of material, too. In each project much of the materials research we do is related to sustainability. Is the material manufactured locally? How is it produced? What's used to produce it?

STEVENSON: When the LEED guidelines first came out we were surprised that the values involved already were our values, and not

Brown University Mind-Brain Building, perspective digital-and-hand sketch in section

necessarily because they are sustainable issues. They're issues about natural light and quality of views, about being able to open windows and using sensible solar orientation that we've incorporated into buildings from the very beginning of our practice, as at the Hanscom Field Maintenance Building (1988). Our desire to build and rebuild in the city, as we have demonstrated with all of the urban Boys and Girls Clubs, is a very sustainable principle. Research into materials is a fresh, ever-changing issue in the green realm.

AB: *How do model making, three-dimensional renderings, and other forms of representation factor into your design process?*

LEERS: While many firms use digital modeling almost exclusively now, we have found that a mix of physical modeling at all scales and digital modeling advance both our own decision-making process and our ability to communicate with our clients.

Each tool tells us something different. The physical models allow us to get a really tangible sense of massing, of material. Digital modeling gets us into spaces, flying around and through them.

STEVENSON: But physical models give a much better feeling for space. A fly though is experiential but not spatial. We need both.

WEINZAPFEL: The photomontage approach that we employ is very useful for a close-scale reading of the place and the development of the architecture.

Massachusetts General Hospital, BIM-based elevation

LEERS: Despite the photorealism that we can achieve in digital modeling, we've found that clients really respond very positively to physical models at all scales. There's something really lovable about little models. In bigger models, clients have a sense of touch, of...

WEINZAPFEL: ...what it's going to be like there.

LEERS: Digital imagery can be frightening to a client who sees it as utterly finished, not in progress, because it looks so real. We also do a lot of mixed media, which provides a lively in-progress feeling. That's really important for clients in terms of representation. It suggests a dynamic process rather than a fixed decision.

WEINZAPFEL: It's important to note that model making in our office continues in the field with full-size mockups, and that is an increasingly important way that we learn about what we've drawn, how it is made, how it is assembled, how it looks. Glass, for example, may have different reflectivity than we'd anticipated because the small models had a different light quality than the mockup.

We all go out into the field. We all fuss over the details. This is not an office where we have the conceptual designers over here, the detailers over there, and the field people in another corner. We are all involved from start to finish.

Brown University Mind-Brain Building, partial exterior facade model at 1/4" = 1'-0"

AB: *Leers Weinzapfel has focused on articulating simple envelopes through refined details. The craft of the detail has been a defining expression of your work. Why?*

WEINZAPFEL: Part of this may have to do with building in New England, where the taut envelope is one that is easy

Brown University Athletic Center, competition digital rendering

to protect against the elements. Another is that we often have tight budgets and we take them very seriously, working within the aspirations of the program and creating a design that can be built.

PRYSE: If you have a simple, cost-effective envelope you can spend more time on the details, but you can't have a complex form and a richly detailed building and maintain a tight budget.

LEERS: There are many reasons why we work with a particular vocabulary of forms, but I think underneath all of that is a sensibility—a minimalism, I would say, and a clarity of form, of elemental form—that is where we begin. That language is in our bones. Speaking from my own roots and the influence of Louis Kahn, that search for the primal form, the most fundamental expression of a use and a volume is where I begin my thinking for each project.

The articulation of those primal shapes and forms, the sensual qualities of their surfaces and materials, that is the very stuff that brings them alive because they're not just diagrams. And all that gets adjusted and modified and developed and refined according to purpose and place.

Human Measure

AB: *How do you elicit sensory responses through spatial and material qualities?*

LEERS: We begin with a deep examination of the fundamental human purpose of a place. We do this through real dialogue with our clients. We observe them in the places they currently occupy and then we look for the fit between that human purpose and experience and its architectural expression. A youth community center wants to be exuberant and playful, like the Blue Hill Avenue Youth Development Center. A university building wants to be a place of lively exchange. A courthouse wants to have a sense of quiet deliberation. For us, the feeling of a space grows out of human occupancy. That's the starting point.

Harvard Science Center, digital rendering

WEINZAPFEL: We want users to clearly understand their buildings. At the same time, we want to heighten their enjoyment of the spaces through light, color, and materials, and also to have a thoughtful engagement with the ideas of the building, which some may experience immediately and others may only attain over time.

LEERS: We're in an era in which there are tremendous innovations and explorations going on with the envelopes of buildings, which is critically important work. But for us, it's never been just about the exterior identity of a building, the form, or the massing. The crafting of spaces, whether they're dynamic or serene, has been a fundamental piece of our work.

Sensory experience of a building really comes from light revealing volumes and textures. The sensory impact of materials—smooth, shiny, rough—is also revealed by light, so light is really the shaper of space and the means by which texture and tactile sensation are revealed.

Fenton Judicial Center, courtroom

For a long period of time procession and movement and hierarchy of space went out the window. But I do think that, once again, in the world of ideas right now, attention is turning to sequence, to a sense of moving through spaces of different qualities.

AB: *What are your priorities in terms of developing spatial sequences that inform users and propel them through a building?*

LEERS: The Fenton Judicial Center (1998) we designed in the city of Lawrence, Massachusetts, sits in a context of nineteenth-century brick textile mills. We made a brick building. That brick comes into the lobby, where it creates a fairly dense and dark public space. We wanted to keep this very active space relatively quiet in terms of color and texture and material. In contrast, the tall maple-clad volumes of the courtrooms provide a burst of illumination, which is uplifting in spirit, and that was one of the ways we choreographed the spatial and textural experience of the program.

AB: *Proportion is a key element of Leers Weinzapfel's work. Please explain the employment of rhythm and harmony in the firm's work.*

Brown University Mind Brain Building, digital rendering of partial exterior facade

WEINZAPFEL: We learned a long time ago that the idea of measure, of the actual size of things and their repetition and their proportional relationship, was fundamental to the way we composed building elements. We've always spent a great deal of time and study on the proportion and shape of spaces, on the legibility of the exterior wall. The difference between a pretty good building and a really beautiful building is that refinement of measure.

STEVENSON: But going back to the ensemble, a lot of times these proportions and rhythms have something to do with our neighbors. Similar cadences and structural bays make the buildings relate to each other in a unique way.

LEERS: And we also use the human body as a measure, as a kind of portrait format in our proportional thinking about space. All of these ideas—measure of proportion, of scale—they're all part of an idea of precision, precision fit in a way. The metaphor of tailoring is apt. The exact size of things and their frequency, subdivision, and modulation is an essential characteristic of our design. Beyond an abstract idea of form, of space, of concept, the careful adjustment of all those things to a true size and measure constitutes an important dimension of our architecture.

Very often when we begin work on a new kind of space, or even a familiar type of space, we study similar projects and note their dimensions, assess what makes them feel right. Is it their length to width to height? Their materials? The direction light enters? This is our field research. It produces data that we use in generating our work.

This is quite a different operation from parametric space making. It is tailoring, not manufacturing. It is the way we work. It's the methodology that will bring us to a humane environment with human measure.

Harvard Science Center, digital corridor study

STUDIO

Project Credits

**University of Pennsylvania Gateway Complex
Philadelphia, PA**
Client: University of Pennsylvania
Leers Weinzapfel Team: Jane Weinzapfel, Principal-in-Charge; Andrea P. Leers, Principal; Joe Raia, Project Manager; Cathy Lassen, Project Architect;
Design Team: Ellen Altman, Tom S. Chung, John Kim, Mee Lee, Anne Snelling-Lee, and Margaret Minor Wood
Consultant Team: Mechanical and Electrical Engineers: Trefz Engineering, Inc.; Structural Engineer: Keast and Hood Co.; Civil Engineer: Boles, Smyth Associates, Inc.; Landscape Architect: Michael Van Valkenburgh Associates; Lighting Designer: Lam Partners
Construction Manager: Sordoni Skanska USA
Awards: Business Week/Architectural Record Award, 2001; the Chicago Athenaeum American Architecture Award, 2001; American Institute of Architects Honor Award, 2001; American Institute of Steel Construction, National Award, 2001; International Association of Lighting Designers Award, 2001; I.D. Magazine Award, 2001; Boston Society of Architects Honor Award, 2000; P/A Citation, 1999

**Princeton University Chilled Water Plant Expansion
Princeton, New Jersey**
Client: Princeton University
Leers Weinzapfel Team: Jane Weinzapfel, Principal-in-Charge; Joe Pryse, Principal and Project Manager; Design Team: Ross Hummel, Justin Lee, Rachel Levitt, and Margaret Minor Wood
Prime Consultant and Lead Engineer: Carter Burgess (currently Jacobs)
General Contractor: Skanska USA
Awards: ACEC New Jersey Engineering Excellence Honor Award, 2007; Texas CEC Engineering Excellence Silver Award, 2007; Boston Society of Architects Honor Award, 2006

**University of Cincinnati University Pavilion
Cincinnati, Ohio**
Client: University of Cincinnati
Leers Weinzapfel Team: Andrea P. Leers, Principal; Jane Weinzapfel, Principal; Joe Pryse, Project Manager; Alex Adkins, Project Architect; Design Team: Ellen Altman, Michael Bardin, Ezekial Brown, Sam Choi, Tom S. Chung; John Kim, Gitte Knupsen, Dan Lamp, Mee Lee, Ralph Plemel, and Randy Whinnery
Associate Architect: GBBN Architects
Consultant Team: Structural Engineer: THP Limited, Inc.; Mechanical, Electrical, and Plumbing Engineers: Fosdick and Hilmer; Civil Engineer: Balke Engineers; Landscape Architect: Bentley Koepke, Inc.; Exhibit Designers: Amaze Design; Lighting Designer: Lam Partners;
General Contractor: Cornell Group; Turner Construction
Awards: Boston Society of Architects Honor Award, 2007

**Blue Hill Avenue Youth Development Center
Boston, Massachusetts**
Client: City of Boston and the Boys and Girls Clubs of Boston
Leers Weinzapfel Team: Andrea P. Leers, Principal-in-Charge; Josiah Stevenson, Design Project Manager; Jim Vogel, Construction Project Manager; Design Team: Natasha Espada and Lisa Schmidt
Associate Architect: Chisholm Washington Associates
Consultant Team: Structural Engineer: LeMessurier Consultants, Inc.; Mechanical, Electrical, and Plumbing Engineers: TMP Consulting Engineers, Inc.; Civil Engineer: Green International Affiliates and Lottero and Mason Associates, Inc.; Landscape Architect: Mary Smith Associates
General Contractor: Boston Building & Bridge Corp.
Awards: American Institute of Architects New England, 1996; Harleston Parker Medal, City of Boston and the Boston Society of Architects, 1996; Boston Society of Architects, 1995

**MIT School of Architecture and Planning Renovations
Cambridge, Massachusetts**
Client: Massachusetts Institute of Technology
Leers Weinzapfel Team: Jane Weinzapfel, Principal-in-Charge; Andrea P. Leers, Principal; Alex Adkins and Joe Raia, Project Managers; Jim Vogel, Specifications; Design Team: Mark Armstrong, Sam Choi, Suzanne Kim, Ute Kupzog, Karen Moore, Cathy Lassen, Mee Lee, Ann Snelling-Lee, Lauren Rockart, Karen Swett, LiLian Tan, and Belinda Watt
Consultant Team: Structural Engineer: Lim Consultants; Electrical Engineer Phase 1–3: Lottero & Mason Associates; Mechanical Engineer Phase 1–3: TMP Consulting Engineers; Mechanical and Electrical Engineers Phase 4–5: Vanderweil Engineers
Construction Manager: Linbeck
Awards: Business Week/Architectural Record Award, 1999; I.D. Magazine Award 1998; American Institute of Architects Honor Award for Interior Architecture, 1998; Interiors Magazine Award, 1997; Boston Society of Architects Honor Award, 1996

**Smith College Fitness Center
Northampton, Massachusetts**
Client: Smith College
Leers Weinzapfel Team: Josiah Stevenson, Principal-in-Charge and Project Manager; Andrea P. Leers, Principal; Design Team: Dominic Passeri, Nicole Perri, Li Lian Tan, and Jim Vogel
Consultant Team: Structural Engineer: LeMessurier Consultants; Mechanical Engineer: M.J. Moran, Inc.; Electrical Engineer: Collins Electric; Civil Engineer: Huntley Associates, P.C.
General Contractor: A.R. Green & Son, Inc.

**Harvard University Science Center Expansion
Cambridge, Massachusetts**
Client: Harvard University
Leers Weinzapfel Team: Andrea P. Leers, Principal in Charge; Jane Weinzapfel, Principal; Winifred Stopps, Project Architect and Project Manager; Alexander Carroll, Project Architect and Project Manager; Design Team: Ellen Altman, Mark Armstrong, Tom S. Chung, Nicolas D'Angelo, Natasha Espada, Rachel Levitt, Paul Stanbrige, Chris Stanley, and Leanne Zilka
Consultant Team: Structural, Mechanical, Electrical, Plumbing, and Fire Protection Engineers: Ove Arup & Partners; Landscape Architect: Stephen Stimson Associates; Acoustical Consultant: Cavanaugh, Tocci Associates, Inc.; Lighting Designer: Berg Howland Associates; Curtain Wall Consultant: R.A. Heintges & Associates
Construction Manager: Linbeck
Awards: International Design Award, Institutional PRO Category awarded to Puches Design for the Putnam Gallery, 2007; the Chicago Athenaeum American Architecture Award, 2006; Boston Society of Architects Honor Award, 2004; American Institute of Architects New England Award, 2004

**Cambridge School of Weston Mugar Center for the Performing Arts
Weston, Massachusetts**
Client: Cambridge School of Weston
Leers Weinzapfel Team: Jane Weinzapfel, Principal-in-Charge; Josiah Stevenson, Principal and Project Manager; Design Team: Ellen Altman, Choi Choon, Natasha Espada, Cathy Lassen, Joe Raia, and Jim Vogel
Consultant Team: Structural Engineer: Lim Consultants; Mechanical, Electrical, and Plumbing Engineer: TMP Consulting Engineers and Lottero & Mason Associates;
Civil Engineer: Green International Affiliates; Landscape Architect: Michael Van Valkeburgh Associates; Theater Consultant: Theatre Projects, Inc.; Acoustical Consultant: Cavanaugh Tocci
General Contractor: Travi Construction
Awards: Boston Society of Architects Honor Award, 2003; The Chicago Athenaeum American Architecture Award, 2001; American Institute of Architects New England Award, 2000

Harvard University New College Theatre
Cambridge, Massachusetts

Client: Harvard University
Leers Weinzapfel Team: Andrea P. Leers, Principal-in-Charge; Josiah Stevenson, Principal; Joe Raia, Project Manager; Matthew Petrie, Project Architect; Design Team: Steven Chaitow, Sam Choi, Nicolas D'Angelo, Min-Chang Lee, Rachel Levitt, Tina Murdough, Susanne Schwokowsky, Chistopher Stanley, Dominic Passeri, and Tiantian Xu
Consultant Team: Structural Engineer: Lim Consultants; Mechanical, Electrical, and Plumbing Engineers: Cosentini Associates; Civil Engineer: Green International Affiliates; Theater Consultant: Fisher Dachs Associates; Lighting Designer: Lam Partners; Acoustical Consultant: Acentech
General Contractor: Shawmut Design and Construction
Awards: Cambridge Historical Commission Preservation Award, 2008; Associated General Contractors Aon Build America Award, 2008; Building Design + Construction Magazine Reconstruction Award—Gold Level, 2007

Harvard University Library Services Building
Cambridge, Massachusetts

Client: Harvard Planning and Real Estate
Leers Weinzapfel Team: Andrea P. Leers, Principal-in-Charge; Jane Weinzapfel, Principal; Natasha Espada, Project Manager and Project Architect; Joe Raia, Project Manager; Design Team: Tom S. Chung, Vaughn Miller, Tom Lee, Tina Murdough, Tina Tollis, Randy Whinnery, and Jim Vogel,
Interiors Architect: Samuel Anderson Architects
Consultant Team: Structural Engineer: Lim Consultants; Mechanical, Electrical, and Plumbing Engineers: Cosentini Associates; Civil Engineer: Green International Affiliates; Landscape Architect: Stephen Stimson Associates; Lighting Designer: Brandston Partnership, Inc.; Acoustical Consultant: Acentech (Core/Shell), Acoustic Dimensions (Tenant Interiors); Geothermal Consultant: Water Energy Distributors, Inc.
Construction Manager: Jackson Construction
Awards: Boston Society of Architects Honor Award, 2008; American Institute of Architects New York Building Type Design Award for Sustainable Design, 2008; LEED Gold Rating, U.S. Green Building Council, 2007; American Institute of Architects New England Merit Award, 2007

U.S. District Courthouse
Orlando, Florida

Client: General Services Administration
Leers Weinzapfel Team: Andrea P. Leers, Principal-in-Charge; Josiah Stevenson, Principal and Project Manager; Jane Weinzpafel, Principal; Design Team: Kelle Brooks, Steven Chaitow, Tom S. Chung, Nicholas D'Angelo, Dominic Passeri, Susanne Schwokowsky, and Tiantian Xu
Joint Venture Partner/Architect: HLM Design-Heery International, Inc.
Consultant Team: Structural, Mechanical, Electrical, Plumbing, and Security Engineers: HLM Design-Heery International, Inc.; Landscape Architect: Office of Dan Kiley; Acoustical Consultant: Cavanagh Tocci
General Contractor: Hensel Phelps Construction Co.
Awards: The Chicago Athenaeum American Architecture Award, 2008; American Institute of Architects Academy of Architecture for Justice Knowledge Community Justice Facilities Review Award, 2008; American Institute of Architects Orlando Award of Excellence, 2008; Retrospective of Courthouse Design Citation, National Center for State Courts, 2001

Andrea P. Leers, FAIA

Andrea P. Leers received a bachelor of arts in art history from Wellesley College and a master of architecture from the Graduate School of Fine Arts at the University of Pennsylvania. Leers founded an independent practice in 1970, and in 1982 she and Jane Weinzapfel established Leers Weinzapfel Associates in Boston, Massachusetts. In 1991 she was elected to the AIA's College of Fellows. In 1997 she was a visiting artist at the American Academy in Rome. In 2007 she was Chaire des Amériques at the University of Paris 1 Panthéon-Sorbonne.

She is currently an adjunct professor of Architecture and Urban Design at the Harvard University Graduate School of Design (GSD) and the former director of the Masters of Urban Design Program. Previous teaching posts include visiting critic at the University of Pennsylvania and Tokyo Institute of Technology, Harry S. Shure Visiting Professor at the University of Virginia, and adjunct associate professor at Yale University. Since 1979, Leers has been involved in research and design in Japan, through which she earned an NEA/ Japan U.S. Friendship Commission Design Arts Fellowship.

Leers is a national leader in courthouse design, having taught the Executive Education Seminar at the GSD since 1993. She currently serves on the U.S. General Services Administration's Public Buildings Service and was formerly a member of the Architectural Advisory Board for the U.S. Department of State. She is a member of the President's Visiting Committee of the Massachusetts Institute of Technology (MIT) School of Architecture and Planning as well as a commissioner for the Boston Civic Design Commission (BCDC), the mayor-appointed committee that reviews all of the city's major development and institutional projects.

Jane Weinzapfel, FAIA

Jane Weinzapfel received a bachelor of architecture from the University of Arizona School of Architecture. After working with a large architecture and planning group, Weinzapfel opened an independent practice in 1980. Two years later, she and Andrea Leers founded Leers Weinzapfel Associates. In 1994 she was elected to the AIA's College of Fellows. In 2002 she was a visiting artist at the American Academy in Rome.

Weinzapfel has taught at the MIT School of Architecture and Planning and is a visiting critic at the University of Arizona College of Architecture and Landscape Architecture, where she served on the dean's advisory board. She has been a juror and speaker at numerous universities. She is a former trustee, board director, and current overseer of the Boston Architectural College.

An expert in transportation and urban infrastructure design, Weinzapfel is a longtime member and former director of the Women's Transportation Seminar. She has also served on the mayor's Advisory Committee on Transportation for Boston, and the mayor's Advisory Committee on City Hall Plaza.

She is a former president and a two-time board director of the Boston Society of Architects and has served on its executive committee. She was a board director of the AIA New England Regional Council; she is a speaker at national and regional AIA conferences. She often acts as speaker and juror for AIA design awards. She has served on the editorial board of *ArchitectureBoston* and the advisory board of *Harvard Design Magazine*. She is a chair of the trustees of Boston by Foot.

Joe Pryse, AIA

Joe Pryse received a bachelor of architecture with distinction from the University of Kentucky, where he was awarded the Dean Anthony Eardley Award for design. He earned a master of architecture from the University of Virginia; while there, he received the Lori Ann Pristo Award and won a Virginia Society of the AIA competition.

Pryse joined Leers Weinzapfel Associates in 1989 and became a principal in 1998. He has led many of the firm's expansion and renovation projects, including Northside Middle School and Schmitt Elementary School (1991) in Columbus, Indiana, and the award-winning Headquarters of the Combined Jewish Philanthropies (1995) in Boston. He directed the work on the University of Cincinnati University Pavilion and was the principal-in-charge of architecture and construction for the MIT Media Arts and Sciences expansion project (2010), a collaboration with the office of Fumihiko Maki and Associates. Pryse has also completed projects at the University of North Carolina and Princeton University.

Pryse has a strong interest in detailing and materials and directs the firm's Quality Control Program. He has taught design studios at the University of Virginia, the Boston Architectural College, and the University of Kentucky Summer School. He has been a guest critic at the New York Institute of Technology, the GSD, Yale University, Roger Williams University, and Wentworth Institute of Technology. He has lectured on the firm's work at Harvard University, MIT, and Wentworth Institute of Technology.

Josiah Stevenson, AIA

Josiah Stevenson received a bachelor of arts from Dartmouth College and a master of architecture from the GSD. He joined Leers Weinzapfel Associates in 1986 and became a principal in 1998.

Stevenson's expertise in athletic, recreation, and campus-life facilities has contributed to many of the firm's community-oriented projects, including the Blue Hill Avenue Youth Development Center (1995), which won the 1996 Harleston Parker Medal from the Boston Society of Architects, and the George Robert White Gymnasium and Teen Center (1991), which received a design award from AIA New England. He coordinates and coteaches, with Leers, The New American Courthouse an executive education course at the GSD. He has researched courtroom prototypes with the Commonwealth of Massachusetts and the Trial Court of the Commonwealth, with the intent to establish the courtroom of the future.

Stevenson is LEED accredited and is very interested in sustainable design and the effects of buildings on their environments. Together with a large group of interested coworkers, he leads the firm's effort in educating, disseminating, and incorporating sustainable-design practices in the office. He has lectured on the firm's work, has taught or participated in final reviews at several New England architecture schools, and has been active as a design reviewer in his hometown of Cohasset, Massachusetts.

Associates

Tom S. Chung, AIA, LEED AP

Natasha Espada, AIA, LEED AP

Joseph M. Raia, AIA, LEED AP

Winifred Stopps, AIA, LEED AP

James E. Vogel, AIA, LEED AP, CSI

Acknowledgments

This book is long overdue. Each time we began to approach the idea of documenting the arc of our work, doing the work intervened. Only when we were honored with the 2007 AIA Architecture Firm Award did we finally realize it was time to give attention to this long-delayed chance to pause, reflect, and look ahead. However, waiting for over twenty-five years to do so means that the task of thanking all of those who contributed along the way is daunting.

Our gratitude must begin with those who nurtured us—teachers, mentors, and wise advisors—whose lessons are with us daily and whose wisdom and example sustains and inspires us. We continue to learn from our professional and faculty colleagues, as well as from our students who challenge us to explore, expand, and persevere in pursuing our deepest held values. We are enormously grateful for the thoughtful and critical perspectives on our work of Joan Busquets and Marion Weiss, which are presented here, as well as for their friendship.

Like all architects, we can only design to our full potential with a great client, and we have been fortunate to work with extraordinary individuals in the community and public sector, at universities and schools, and in the business world. They all share a curiosity about the world of architecture, the willingness to learn from us, and the desire to teach us in the long and often arduous process of developing a project.

Our consultants are critical partners in our design, and the ability to work closely and creatively with them is absolutely fundamental to our own thinking process. We thank them, as well as the many fine contractors whose commitment to realizing our vision in craft and working along side us is exceptional.

Of course, our studio group is the heart of our collaboration, and we share the credit for the work presented in this book with all the people who have contributed to our projects over the years. We would particularly like to recognize our present and former associates, our administrative staff, and the many friends and supporters who have shared our passion for design and for an inclusive and collaborative workplace.

Special thanks to the many people who contributed to *Made to Measure*: Abby Bussel, whose editorial guidance for both text and graphics was remarkable; Gabrielle Angevine and Kevin Bell, who organized and managed this book project despite enormous other demands on their time; and Hung-Yang Chien, Juliet Chun, Stephen Fan, Billy Glick, Patrick Hamon, Shih Min Hsu, Julie Janeo, and Jared Ramsdell, who created drawings and diagrams that should have been done long ago, but are finally available to complete the story of our work so far. A final thanks goes to our editors and graphic designer at Princeton Architectural Press for their enthusiasm and guidance on this project.

Illustration Credits

Published by
Princeton Architectural Press
37 East 7th Street
New York, NY 10003

For a free catalog of books, call 1-800-722-6657
Visit our website at www.papress.com

Editors: Wendy Fuller and Linda Lee
Designer: Paul Wagner

Special thanks to: Bree Anne Apperley, Sara Bader,
Nicola Bednarek Brower, Janet Behning, Megan Carey, Becca
Casbon, Carina Cha, Tom Cho, Penny (Yuen Pik) Chu, Russell
Fernandez, Pete Fitzpatrick, Jan Haux, John Myers, Katharine
Myers, Dan Simon, Andrew Stepanian, Jennifer Thompson,
Joseph Weston, and Deb Wood of Princeton Architectural Press
—Kevin C. Lippert, publisher

Library of Congress Cataloging-in-Publication Data
Leers, Andrea.
Made to measure : the architecture of Leers Weinzapfel
Associates / Andrea Leers. — 1st ed.
    p.   cm.
ISBN 978-1-56898-957-0 (alk. paper)
1. Leers Weinzapfel Associates. 2. Architecture—United
States—History—20th century. 3. Architecture—United States—
History—21st century. I. Title.
NA737.L425A4 2010
720.92'2—dc22
                                    2010025388